RIGHTING THE WRONG

Closing the Gender Gap *in* Computing

Frances Grundy

Lulu Publishing Services rev. date: 08/29/2020

DEDICATION

To my father David William Donaldson DSO* DFC (1915 – 2004) who served throughout the Second World War fearlessly and with constant diligence. Subsequently in civilian life he provided me with endless support and sound advice in my endeavours to improve the lot of women.

ACKNOWLEDGMENTS

The idea for this collection was originally suggested by Debora Weber-Wulff and I am indebted to her and to Irene Glendinning for their continued support and input of ideas. I also owe many colleagues much gratitude for the time and patience they spent reading and commenting on my contributions over the years and of these I would especially like to thank Eva Turner who has contributed much time and many comments in the preparation of this collection. Thanks go to Ursula Rutherford who so competently proofread the manuscript. Discussing the design of the cover with the artist Greg Genestine-Charlton was an education in itself. I hadn't realised how prosaic and pedestrian my view of drawing and design was until he kept telling me 'It's whatever you want to see in it'.

Finally, I would like to pay tribute to John Grundy (who I'm sure would have been appreciative of the cover design and with whom I would have intensely enjoyed discussing it). For all the years I was writing these I benefited from his encouragement and his tenacity in helping me unravel knots. I could never have completed this work if I had not had the advantages of his expertise in moral philosophy, his clarity of thought, his patience, his skill with words and willingness to help me think what in computing circles was the unthinkable. The ideas would still be buzzing around my head in an inarticulate mass driving me mad!

CONTENTS

PART IV: CHANGE?

PART V: INTERDISCIPLINARITY AND OTHER APPROACHES

FOREWORD FROM SUE BLACK

I set up BCSWomen, the UK's first online network for women in tech, back in 1998 with the aim of supporting and encouraging women in tech and providing a space for us to discuss technology online as we didn't often get the chance to meet each other face to face. I've had a great time over the last 21 years championing women in tech, meeting so many wonderful women and seeing students that I've encouraged go on to have successful careers. It's great to see now the proliferation of women's and girls' tech initiatives not just in the UK but all over the world, I feel very happy to have played a small part in helping to make that happen.

I've only been able to do what I've done because I've stood on the shoulders of giants, an important one of whom is Frances Grundy. Frances has been studying and researching the area of women in tech for some thirty years having started working in the computing industry in the mid-1960s. She was banging the drum for more women in computing before I went to university. A thought pioneer, Frances has not only challenged and led thinking in this area but provides us with research to help guide us in creating a more equal and just world. This book brings together Frances' lifetime's work in one place, it takes us on a journey through a career and also through decades of thought and analysis. I highly recommend this wide ranging collection of papers to anyone interested in equality and diversity, particularly in the area of women in technology.

Professor Sue Black OBE
Durham University

FOREWORD FROM
BRITTA SCHINZEL

Having known and accompanied my friend, the computer scientist Frances Grundy, on an academic journey through several decades working with her pursuing scientific and gender political activities, I am delighted to contribute this foreword to her second book. She twice spent time as a guest at my Institute for Computer Science and Social Research and Gender Studies in Computing and Science at the University of Freiburg, where she gave courses on Gender Studies in Computing. I remember being particularly impressed by a workshop in which she applied Critical Discourse Analysis to texts in computing.

I am delighted to see collected into this new volume her feminist texts on Computing and related matters that were not included in her earlier book *Women and Computers* published in 1996. The result is impressive: a broad variety of topics from the field of gender and computing arising during the span of her professional life, plus a new text on teaching and another new chapter written in 2018 asking 'Just How Much Has Changed?'. In ten chapters Grundy deals with the subject of Computer Science from many different viewpoints: its development as part of the technology of war, its emergence from mathematics and engineering, the subsequent development of software production, human-computer interaction and the situation of professionals and of women in IT. In a sequence of chapters (Chapters 3, 4 and 5) she places under the overarching discipline of gender studies the relationship between computing and engineering, along with mathematics, science and the consequences of the history of these disciplines for women from early computing until the present day. These and other chapters deal with the genealogy of computing and its consequential relationship to mathematics and engineering and the role of interdisciplinarity not only between these three subjects, but also between computing and other subjects within the humanities, sociology and philosophy. The theme of the influence of these origins of computing and its subsequent development is something Grundy often raises. Their masculine base, as it were, and the lack of realisation of their influence is part and parcel of the present situation.

Indeed, in the final chapter 'Working at the Boundaries' (Chapter 10) Grundy examines the nature of interdisciplinary boundaries and the permeability of these boundaries, both concerning the objects of study and objects of discourse that have emerged at these boundaries and at their interstices. She mourned then, in 2004, the fact that there were so few institutes or schools that bridged technology and other disciplines (beyond the one she was working in) and now, in 2020, there doesn't appear to have been that much change.

In chapter 8, 'Time in the Gender-Technology Relationship', she notes how the ever-accelerating speed of technological change can affect women and men differently.

Many of the chapters start with an in-depth consideration of the history of computers and computing with respect to the current topic. Her methodological approach is therefore first a historical one – in some cases using established gender theories, such as aspects of gender suggested by Sandra Harding in 1986: gender structure, gender symbolism and gender identity or individual gender. Some of her investigations use discourse and text analysis.

Chapter 2 on teaching computing and IT education is a new addition. As the optimum age range to introduce children to IT is between two and seven years, it is necessary to stimulate children's emotions. Instead of using computers to solve simple tasks within routine learning, the suggestion now is that children should be encouraged to use their inspiration in coding to solve problems following their own personal and diverse interests. Analogously Grundy's proposal is to awake and hold older students' interests, and to prepare them for the rapid and frequent innovations typical of the discipline. She very rightly demands that teaching should comprise the history of computing, ethics and gender in STEM and in the work force at large, it should put students in a mind-set to think analytically and to move fluently between disciplines.

In Chapter 6, 'Women, Power and Progress', Grundy uses Michel Foucault's analyses of power to examine how power operates in our modern world. She illustrates this analysis using a relevant example in the world of employment showing how this modern version of power can be used to hinder, or indeed stop, women's progress.

The penultimate chapter 'Just How Much Has Changed?' reviews some achievements of women in science and the conditions in which they worked through the last three centuries. It then turns to what is happening in the 21st century. And, in spite of widespread knowledge of what women could achieve, the reasons for women's reluctance to get into and, more importantly, stick with Computing and IT, the situation remains very much the same. The situation is confounded further by, for example, the lack of intersectional analysis which would reveal further problems for non-white and LGBTQ+ women. Too many women imagine they have equal access to opportunities and equal rights thanks to legal institutions and workplace regulations; in practice, as Michel Foucault maintained, they don't. It's a myth.

Grundy's collection of wide-ranging essays taken with her earlier book (that she began writing in 1990) illustrate just how far we haven't come in three decades in spite of all the work so many of us have done and the angst we have suffered at the hands of the dominant nay-sayers. Her range of work pointing to all that has been done culminating in the final chapter in this volume suggests nothing is going to change unless we rethink our approach to this gender disparity in such an all-important discipline. We should take heed of Mary Beard's suggestion – not forgetting Michel Foucault – and think harder and more deeply about the nature of power – where it comes from and how it is exercised.

Frances and I are both retired now, as are many of our colleagues. We hope that new generations will see all that has been done and will learn from it.

Professor Dr. Britta Schinzel
Freiburg im Breisgau

CHAPTER 1

INTRODUCTION

THE OBJECT OF THIS book is to alert readers to the long and seemingly everlasting failure of computer and closely allied professions to comprehend and rectify the paucity of women in the industry.

The first part, Part I **The Current Situation**, illustrates this assertion with some statistics from the UK. It has to be observed that, in spite of these depressing figures, we all regularly see girls and boys enjoying social media on their phones and making good, and sometimes not so good, use of technology. How many girls aged 10 or so have we seen teaching not just their grandparents but also their parents the technicalities of taking videos on their phones? Women do so much clerical work operating online systems with skill and perhaps sometimes boredom.

However, and this is a big 'however', these people are making use of what they are given. They are rarely found working at the sharp end where new ideas, for example in the field of artificial intelligence (AI) and other technical innovations, are developed. For the major part the book relies on old papers which serve to illustrate how we have arrived at this situation. The points made in these papers have been made for years and little heed has been taken.

The bulk of this book is in three parts. Following the introductory Part I, Part II examines the **Foundations of Computing**. The common mantra is that computing is based on Science, Engineering and Mathematics or a combination of these. True indeed and there is no getting away from this. But the emphasis on these descriptions has had a severe effect on women's perception of this subject. As with so many themes, like racism and sexism, people absorb fragments of attitudes from many, many sources as they mature. They need to become aware of what they are ingesting and for the most part probably not questioning.

The three papers comprising Part II Chapters 3–5, were all written at the turn of the century. They received little comment at the time but the points raised remain valid. These documents itemise some historical masculine influences; influences that emanate from what is taught, how it is taught and how and where it is ultimately practised. The three disciplines mentioned have always had, and still have, a predominance of male practitioners and, just as importantly, are controlled largely by men. Given the relative novelty of the computing discipline at the time these papers were written, and the prevailing sexism, the absence of opportunities for women was unlikely to be addressed. And it wasn't – by anybody. Computer scientists were too busy building new, better and more exciting systems. And those in charge always knew best.[1] Even now lip service is paid to the interests of women and girls, I have fairly recently watched academic videos on YouTube of well-respected men lecturing with the same assurance to a predominantly male audience. They made no mention whatsoever of the problem. It's still as if there is no problem. (Peyton Jones 2016)

So these papers are being aired again. Everyone should read them and realise (and perhaps relive) what went before. Those governing the direction of computing must realise that it is up to them to ensure that the best brains determine the future. It's not women who have to adjust their approach, but men. Women should scarcely notice it is happening.

Sources of Power is the title for Part III. Having spelt out some of the historical influences the next step is to see how these influences work in practice. In fact throughout Part II there is no reference as to the exact mechanisms as to how these influences are fed to new recruits, although one can perhaps infer a few.

How does power work? Michel Foucault wrote about power and, more recently, Mary Beard has too. If we knew better how power works, how much easier life would be!

The first chapter in Part III entitled *Women, Power and Progress* (Chapter 6) was written later than those in Part II. I was clearly beginning to realise that it wasn't a simple matter just to express severe dissatisfaction with the *status quo* either in written or spoken word, more was needed. I suppose I fell for Michel Foucault while working in Vienna in 2002 and was certainly later chided for it by a fellow activist in this field. But his writings did offer me some possible explanations – and tentative solutions. Foucault wasn't a great feminist but he certainly propounded ideas which are relevant and helpful to feminists asking questions about power.

There are many factors which influence an individual as to which, if any, computing course they decide to enrol on: school, friends, parents and advertising. All these are sources of power. The second chapter in this section (Chapter 7) concentrates on the last: advertising.

One important form of advertisement is the university and departmental prospectus. Although a study of prospectuses probably comes after the general subject area is decided upon, it is important to recognise the detail incorporated in these texts and the influences they may have. Critical discourse analysis is a technique for analysing power relations within texts and against a background of other texts. There may well be features in these texts which are not immediately obvious that 'subterraneously' act to deter women. This chapter (7) describes such an analysis of two university computing prospectuses. The paper that formed the basis for this chapter was written in the late 1990s and references printed texts when on-line prospectuses were not as widely available and used as they are now. The earlier analysis suggested that these printed texts were more sympathetic to women. Later analysis suggests that the online advertisements appeared less sympathetic to women students.

Given the time lapse since this study was undertaken it is true and unsurprising that authors of these texts now incorporate more acceptable presentations, but (as I am reliably informed by colleagues still working in this field) there are plenty of other ideas that those keen to attract women could well take note of. Nonetheless this analysis does serve to emphasise the hegemonic power that was then at work in at least one computing department, a department which is still offering degrees with the same name and still remains high in the 2020 computer science league table. Many of the emphases detrimental to women that occur in these texts are still present in the equivalent modern texts whether on paper or online.

Part IV is about **Change**. What change one might legitimately ask? Chapter 8 entitled, *Time in the Gender Technology Relationship*, was written earlier in 2001. It focusses on how so many of us have to spread our energies and when the crunch comes are frequently left supporting the whole structure in place (households, multi-generational families and so on) when we could be doing more to further our careers. Men do help more than they used to but, by and large, have not yet grasped the full extent of what women do and what they will need to do to make the distribution of this load truly equal.

Chapter 9 is in a sense a 'catch up' chapter in which I recently returned to my life's employment after 15 years of distance from it all. First, I take a long overview of what has happened to women in STEM (Science, Technology, Engineering and Mathematics) and its related disciplines since the seventeenth century. It identifies features of their lives which are relevant for the way in which things (gender pay differentials, being silenced, ridicule) happen to women today. This overview reaches into the present; there is reference to and some detail of events happening now. It is no coincidence that we have ended up with so few women in computing – it was, I suggest, inevitable if steps weren't taken to prevent it. How much change has there been? Superficially there's been a lot in terms of technical advances and women do have many more skills. But there is still a huge gap waiting to be closed.

Interdisciplinarity and its relevance for closing the gender gap in computing is the focus for Part V. Valuing and upgrading interdisciplinarity is possibly one way out of this impasse. The discipline of computing is still relatively young. It attracted much interest during and following the Second World War but for many years lacked the confidence to claim for itself a position in the academic hierarchy. As we have seen in Part II, different authors have for decades claimed different allegiances to engineering, science and mathematics. As taught and practised in universities and academic institutions it can now be regarded as a discipline in its own right and with its own boundaries. But it needs more than that if it is to broaden its appeal and intake.

Chapter 10, *Working at the Boundaries*, examines the nature of disciplines, their boundaries and what can occur where these boundaries meet and are permeated. Sometimes new 'objects of study', as Foucault termed them, are created. Two such objects mentioned in this chapter are plate tectonics and DNA. AI (Artificial Intelligence) and GIS (Geographic Information Systems) are further examples which can be quoted where computing has permeated other disciplinary boundaries. This process of identifying objects of study doesn't necessarily create new disciplines.

All the examples mentioned above are links between 'hard sciences' where the boundaries are notoriously porous. No 'real scientist' feels any embarrassment collaborating with other 'real scientists'.

But, as I go on to argue in this final chapter, interdisciplinarity should occur not only between the 'hard sciences' and computing on the one hand but also between these 'hard' sciences and all kinds of social sciences. Computing is 'man-made'; it is socially constructed and we need to examine the ramifications of this in terms of gender. As well as 'objects of study' Foucault suggested another type of object: 'objects of discourse'. His prime example for this is madness and how it came to be defined at the intersection of the planes of the judiciary, medicine and the police creating a space in which mental illness is defined.

Foucault's discussion doesn't necessarily provide all that much guidance for what we are looking for here; the topic of mental health is just too big. But what we are seeking is not objects of study, we have found those easily enough AI, GIS and so on. What we are seeking is more an object of discourse: the interaction and overlap between this 'manufactured' subject 'computing' on the one hand and 'gender' on the other. What is happening where these two planes intersect? What are the different things happening to women and to men at the intersection? Why are their reactions so different? Both planes are likely to be fragmented into sub-planes; can the sub-planes be identified? For example, a set of sub-planes might be revealed by using intersectionality techniques. Do different groups of women (from different races, ethnicities, cultures and/or from different socio-economic backgrounds) react in different ways to the technological problems they are presented with?

The reluctance of computing academics and practitioners to conduct self-examination is hinted at in the earlier chapters of this book, and this reluctance which occurs in the other disciplines is now revived in this current chapter in relation to computing. This self-examination requires using the techniques of social sciences to look much harder at the detailed impact of these teaching programmes on young women and men with the object of raising national and international awareness. Such studies are indeed currently completed and documented, journals devoted to such topics exist, but the results continue to get lost. It is of paramount importance that all teachers at all levels are made vitally aware of what's happening. Teaching programmes need root and branch reform and ideally should not be conducted primarily by traditional computer scientists. It has to be a subject in its own right.

Such a well-publicised, well-understood interdisciplinary topic on the roots of gender disparity in computing is only a first step.

I return now to objects of study rather than objects of discourse.

The acronym STEAM has been introduced to denote the fields of science, technology, engineering, art (the arts in many different forms) and mathematics (including applied mathematics). It denotes a group of educational programmes designed to encourage students to use the technological and mathematical base that computing provides to think critically and imaginatively about designs and creative approaches to real-world problems. Just including 'art' in this list (which differentiates it from STEM) in no way solves this problem but it does hint at a wider approach where all computing students will remain aware of their foundation subjects and the constraints.

Inspiring students in the foundation topics is critical. Once they have this foundation, then they may be inspired to achieve goals like those suggested in the previous paragraph. What we are trying to do here is not just establish a world-wide understanding of the problem but to emphasise attractive new developments such as the recent, spectacularly popular Esports Fortnite World Cup, and in doing so point young people towards how and where they can get involved in writing and designing these electronic sports activities.

I am seeking for computing graduates to be so well grounded and fired up that when new applications present themselves students seek social and technical solutions in tandem. All this is not to say that there hasn't been a multitude of computer applications in all sorts of spheres for decades. I myself worked on a computer application in Operational Research (mathematics and other disciplines) in the mid-1960s, but at that time computing and mathematics were so deeply entwined nobody really noticed the interdisciplinary aspects of this.

Paradoxically, my own experience was the reverse of what I am seeking. I had enjoyed studying mathematics enormously, in fact avidly in spite of all I have to say about mathematics teaching. At that time computer courses were not generally available – so, when I was offered a job where I could learn computing 'on the hoof' I eagerly accepted it – and then went on to work in computing. But in this case, it was mathematics that inspired me as it did many other female colleagues around that time. I want computing to inspire young – and old.

To have excluded women on the scale it has seems to define the subject of computing as one where women are not welcome and, moreover, one on which they should not be allowed to embark. Yes, computer technology is now a critical part of our lives so it must be fully embraced, but there must be a change informed by how we have got here and a movement alert to what can be done about inclusivity and structure. Right from the earliest level of education there should be a radical rethink of methods and modes of presentation of the subject aimed quite explicitly to engage and immerse more girls and women.

PART I
THE CURRENT SITUATION

CHAPTER 2

TEACHING COMPUTING AND BEYOND

2.1   How to Attract the Very Young?

THERE IS A HUGE unaddressed problem about how to attract the very young. So this isn't about where things have gone wrong; it's about why things haven't really started. We must discover what satisfaction computing technology can give, both in terms of technological creativity and in using technology for enjoyable visionary purposes.

Dame Stephanie Shirley suggested in a Guardian report (Devlin 2017) that "engaging very young children – in particular girls – could ignite a passion for puzzles and problem-solving long before the 'male geek' stereotype took hold". Most children enjoy brain teasers so we need to provide more stimulation for girls to get engaged in puzzles and to devise puzzles themselves. Shirley further noted how evidence suggests that the optimum age range to introduce children to simple coding activities is between two and seven years.[2]

So much of early computing education has until fairly recently been centred on using software to achieve fairly mundane tasks and effectively meant learning by rote. Clearly, such learning procedures have been a problem and therefore often counterproductive providing little or no spark to inspire children's emotions. But in spite of this some children do find things which light up for them within these rule-bound subjects, often depending no doubt on the context, the teacher and the child herself. There are a number of downloadable tools now available to assist people trying to help young children.[3]

In order to identify what might excite more young girls, it might be worth trying to recall what excited us about a subject when we were young, not necessarily very young. For me it was quite late (aged eleven, say) but it was the satisfaction of seeing simple algebraic formulae 'work' – somehow, suddenly, things fell into place and "I could do it". It was about learning rules but it still stuck and most probably shaped my future. But surely what is needed is analysis, recognition and the facility to detect what inspires the very young, girls and boys, and more imagination to tie that into computing activities.[4]

Girls come too late to the subject; the masculine background has already given so many boys a ready advantage and created a world in which girls, for all the usual reasons lack of confidence etc., find it impossible to intervene.

The following and subsequent sections are not about the very young but about primary, secondary school education and later higher education.

2.2 UK Computing Education by the Early 2000s

In schools in the UK (and elsewhere) computing had developed in an ad-hoc manner for a number of reasons. Computers were more or less available to students in their classrooms. But there was no established curriculum and following on from that a shortage of skilled and trained teachers. Teachers from other disciplines were seconded to teach what became labelled as Information, Computing and Technology (ICT) in which students could acquire a GCSE qualification. This ad-hoc development was not the fault of any party, it simply arose. The machines could be used relatively easily to teach basic technical skills like word processing, spreadsheets and so on. Some children were acquiring these skills by themselves outside the schools. There was also a GCSE qualification in Computing and for the post 16-year olds at AS and A-level.

So, we'll start with primary and secondary computing education in the United Kingdom. (In some respects Scotland has slightly different systems to other parts of the UK but these differences are not of importance here.) It is necessary to provide a brief summary of the examinations and their nomenclature. Primary and secondary education run from 5 years old to 16 years old. At the end of secondary education children take a GCSE or General Certificate of Secondary Education. After this they may go on to take Advanced Subsidiary level (AS-level) or Advanced level (A-level) examinations. AS-level is, or may be, the first component of an A-level examination.

A-levels or equivalent vocational qualifications are required for University entrance.

2.3 The New Curriculum

It became clear that children learning ICT were not learning to develop ideas; everything had become concentrated on acquiring this technical proficiency. Over a period of years from 2008 to 2014 a new school curriculum was developed; this was particularly designed to encourage less emphasis on the purely technical and more on creativity in computing. One objective was to encourage ideas relating to all aspects of computing from those closest to hardware to the most esoteric software. This new curriculum, introduced in 2014, aimed to educate all pupils aged 6 through to 16 in the fundamentals of the discipline called 'Computer Science'. The new curriculum has three defined areas: Computer Science, Information Technology and Digital Literacy. Many of the topics appearing amongst these fundamentals are those of computer science as taught in UK universities.

Following the realisation that reform to the existing computing curriculum was needed the Royal Society (instigated by and with support from other bodies, see below) produced an initial report formalising these ideas: *Shut down or restart? The way forward for computing in UK schools* (Royal Society 2012). It is worth noting just how gender bias is addressed in this early report. It is briefly mentioned in an early chapter of the report (Chapter 1, p.15), however under the section headed 'Research Commissioned' immediately following this mention there was no obvious request for research into gender bias or imbalance. At least one respondent to the initial request for evidence for this report expressed serious concern about gender imbalance. There was a section on gender imbalance (Chapter 2, p.13) particularly in relation to entry to Computing A-level but there was no further analysis of this phenomenon. Moreover, the recommendations made no mention of gender. The question had not then really been raised.

There was increased mention of the issues in a subsequent report from the Royal Society *After the Reboot* (Royal Society 2017). Amongst the twelve recommendations there are two which refer to gender: one suggesting investigations into how to improve female participation rates and the other suggesting that 'Government and industry-funded interventions should prioritise and evaluate their impact on improving the gender balance of computing'. But all this fails to address the question as to why the genders are so imbalanced nor does it make any suggestions for realistic achievable actions.

2.3.1 Computing at School CAS

Much of the impetus for this change came from a group of individuals concerned about the lack of direction in computing education. This group, Computing at School CAS (CAS 2018), was formed in 2008 and prompted reviews such as the 2012 report by the Royal Society in addition to support and input from the BCS - The Chartered Institute for IT (*BCS* 2018).

What CAS now offers

It was not just those at the centre who realised something needed changing; many teachers and parents nationwide did too. CAS is now a grass-roots organisation with over 200 regional 'hubs' through which activists keen to improve computing education can meet, talk and exchange ideas. It provides assistance and advice for teachers learning to teach computing anew and for those who have to do it alongside their 'day job'. It has been instrumental in supporting and underpinning the implementation of the 2014 curriculum.

CAS supports many diverse activities mainly focussed on teaching but also providing support for parents. There are, for example, numerous resources for primary and secondary pupils, a Master teacher scheme to provide training for other teachers, a Tenderfoot Programme for continuing professional development (CPD), access to scholarships for teaching and a journal (*Hello World* 2018). There is also a qualification, BCS Certificate in Computer Science Teaching, to certify teachers as proficient in the subject and its pedagogy. The regional structure means that teachers needing advice can access advice locally for free. It is a collaborative venture which almost anyone can join with members freely giving advice which works in collaboration with the BCS and is part of the BCS Academy.

However, it must be said that there is no obvious emphasis on appealing to girls or explicitly addressing the gender gap.

2.4 Gender Statistics for GCSE 2015–2017

Teaching on the new curriculum started in 2016 with the first examinations sat in 2018. The top section in Table 2.1 below shows that while more girls (over 100% more) took GCSE computing in 2016 than in 2015 the numbers were still low at 20% and changed a little in 2017.

Girls who took these subjects performed disproportionately

well, with 25.4% of those who took computing exams achieving top grades (vs. 19.6% of boys) in 2017 (Bennett 2017).

Overall statistics show that the number of pupils taking GCSE computing almost doubled over this period and at the same time ICT as a GCSE subject dropped by almost 35%. (See also (Information Age 2016).) It is worth noting however that the proportions of females taking ICT were relatively high ranging from almost 40% to 42%.

GCSE Computing and ICT	No of Females	% Females	% Females failed
GCSE Computing 2015	5678	16.%1	1.5%
GCSE Computing 2016	12528	20.0%	3.4%
GCSE Computing 2017	13232	19.8%	2.8%
GCSE ICT 2015	47157	42.1%	1.6%
GCSE ICT 2016	34127	40.5%	2.0%
GCSE ICT 2017	28465	38.9%	1.7%
A-level Computing and ICT			
GCE A-Level Computing 2015	456	8%	3.7%
GCE A-Level Computing 2016	609	9.8%	3.3%
GCE A-Level Computing 2017	816	10.0%	4.8%
GCE A-Level ICT 2015	3254	35.7%	2.0%
GCE A-Level ICT 2016	3124	35.8%	2.0%
GCE A-Level ICT 2017	2486	32.7%	2.3%

Table 2.1 Female' results at GCSE and A-level (2015-2017) for all UK candidates (JCQ 2018)

2.4.1 Do Girls Continue with their Computing Studies?

Students may follow on from GCSE level to advanced levels: AS and A-level computing. The former is usually a one-year course whereas an A level is a more advanced course which may take two years. An A-level qualification is more likely to lead to University entrance.

ICT courses were also offered at A and AS level up until 2018.

Teaching to the new syllabus for GCSE commenced in 2016. The syllabus for A and AS level was revised to follow on from this new GCSE syllabus and a new A-level syllabus introduced in 2017. So Table 2.1 shows the results of a mixed collection of syllabuses from which it is not possible to draw conclusions about whether there is a change in attitude amongst girls about the new GCSE, which might have resulted in an increased take up at A-level.

All that can be said is that there is a big leakage between GCSE and AS and A-level. Figures of 16–20% for girls taking GCSE Computing drops to 10% for girls taking A-level Computing.

Also, it appears to be becoming increasingly unpopular. If we now focus on A-level because this qualification is one which can lead to University entrance then the drop from approximately 20% to 10% is serious.[5]

Numbers are low, the leakage is high (Bennett 2017) – what can we examine to see what can be rectified?

2.4.2 The Title 'Computer Science'

The syllabuses show that although Computing is now accepted as the main title for the subject, the core of computing is 'computer science'. In fact computer science is now the only subject that can be taken at this level; "'Harmful' ICT curriculum is set to be dropped to make way for rigorous computer science". (Gov.UK DfE 2012)

The term 'computer science' is used too for AS and A-level syllabus:

> AS and A level specifications in computer science must encourage students to develop: an understanding of, and the ability to apply, the fundamental principles and concepts of computer science, including abstraction, decomposition, logic, algorithms and data representation ...(Gov.UK DfE 2014)

So, it would seem that the science paradigm having gained a strong foothold in universities, schools have now adopted it. And there is a Department for Education document entitled 'Computer science/GCSE Subject Content' (Gov.UK DfE 2015).

As I observe in the next chapter this has been used for decades in many universities and there was some debate in the 1990s which is noted in that chapter. When the GCSE curriculum was revised for the 'reboot' in 2014 this label was accepted without further debate or any research into whether it deters young people from pursuing the subject: girls and women in particular of course but it could also deter boys. Identifying and releasing whatever constraints exist is part of what changing computing education should be about. The distribution of power makes such changes difficult. The university academic structure is still dominated largely by men trained in the culture that had its roots in post war developments (as I discuss in Chapter 9) where the absence of women was unnoteworthy. Bringing influence to bear on this culture is hard – it has of course been extremely successful by its own standards – an elite still presides.

To deride proposals that suggest to some a reduction in the rigour of the discipline, whether or not it is a fact, without carefully analysing the impact of the change should be resisted. At the meta level of teaching, for example deciding on subject titles, course titles, care and wide consultation are required.

2.5   Educational Activities for Girls

2.5.1   Girls Who Code

Unlike CAS which primarily addresses teachers, *Girls Who Code* (Saujani 2018) was founded in 2012 with a single mission: 'to close the gender gap in technology'.

This is a vibrant US organisation whose aim is to encourage girls to enter computing and go on to major in computer science. Sponsored by major tech companies it runs courses across the US, and supports clubs for girls nationwide. In 2020 it had reached more than 50,000 girls in all 50 states. Their website notes clearly the decreasing proportion of female computer scientists in the US since 1995 when it was 37% and is now down to 24% and predicted to go lower still if nothing is done. Consequently, there is a prevailing theme running through the website that things have to change for girls.

There are free after-school programs nationwide in the US and summer courses for 6th-12th grade (age 11 through 18) for girls, and summer immersion training courses are available free at campuses nationwide. The theme of projects covered is wide: ranging from informing students about lead poisoning to destigmatising menstruation.

The mix of topics in all their programmes demonstrates the extent to which other disciplines can enter the computer science arena.

2.5.2 Books

Girls Who Code has published a series with their encouraging overarching title, for example:

Girls Who Code: Learn to Code and Change the World' (Saujani 2017) 'Whether you're a girl who's never coded before, a girl who codes, or a parent raising one, this entertaining book, . . . will have you itching to create your own apps, games, and robots to make the world a better place.'

And there are books of fiction too.

The prevailing theme running through all these activities is one in which girls are at the forefront and they can be confident that their ideas matter and will be considered.

More Books

There are some books for children on Ada Lovelace (more information on her attitude to work and her life appears later in this book in Sections 5.2 and 9.1):

Ada Lovelace (Little People, BIG DREAMS) by Isabel Sanchez Vegara and Zafouko Yamamoto for ages 5–8

Ada Lovelace, Poet of Science: The First Computer Programmer by Diane Stanley and Jessie Hartland for ages 4–8

Ada Lovelace: The Computer Wizard of Victorian England (Who Was...?) by Lucy Lethbridge for age 10+

2.6 Higher Levels of Education

Moving on now to University level, Table 2.2 shows the percentages and numbers of women enrolling on first degree STEM courses and Table 2.3 shows the percentages and numbers of women graduating from first degree courses in all UK institutions for Higher and Further Education (HE and FE). The data for Engineering and Mathematics are included for comparison. Data for Mathematical Sciences show that the take-up by women is good, in fact ranging from 38% to just over 40% between 2014/5 and 2016/7. The main observation to make here is that the percentages are very low for both computer science and engineering.

There is a very limited amount that can be said about continuity of study for cohorts of students moving from computing in secondary education to higher education. There are a number of likely reasons for this including the fact that students can enrol on Computer Science courses in HE without A-Level computing although they can enrol with other A-levels.[6] It is also the case that Scottish data are not included for the GCSE and GCE tables, although they are included for HE.

Tables 2.2 and 2.3 show that the percentages of women enrolling and qualifying on these courses remain about the same throughout the period. (Mathematics has a consistently higher rate of female participation.)

Subject of Study	2014-5	2015-6	2016–7
Computer Science	15.2%	14.9%	17.0%
Engineering & Technology	15.0%	15.7%	16.1%
Mathematical Sciences	38.2%	37.6%	37.4%

Table 2.2: Percentages of women enrolling on first degree courses in UK 2014/15–2016/17 (HESA 2018b)

Subject of Study	2014–5	2015–6	2016–7
Computer Science	17.3%	16.2%	16.1%
Engineering & Technology	15.6%	15.6%	15.8%
Mathematical Sciences	41.0%	39.9%	39.5%

Table 2.3: Percentages of women qualifying on first degree courses in UK 2014/15–2016/17 (HESA 2018a)

2.7 New Approaches to Teaching

This is unquestionably one of the most important areas which needs to be addressed and, given the current power structures which are discussed in the penultimate chapter, the most difficult.

The underlying problem of men's and boys' well rooted dominance in so many aspects of life, particularly things scientific and technical, dominates this issue of altering educational bias and making it seem almost intractable.

At a general level the objectivity associated with scientific thinking can promote rather rigid teaching techniques particularly in a relatively young discipline slightly unsure of itself. So, I suggest an approach to teaching which I call 'interactionism' a challenge in this field of computing to the rather doctrinaire approach that can prevail. With such an approach clearly there is much more exchange of ideas and expressions of misunderstandings with the class.

At a micro level there are some fairly simple solutions which can be applied. Using such clichés in prospectuses as 'aspiring students must be good at maths' or 'Must be good at abstract thinking' won't stir anybody. Packing all the mathematics into a single course doesn't help anybody either. Topics could include, for example, alerting students to the impact of technology on society at large, the history of women in technology, equality and feminist theory and gender power relationships. Why not include within teaching programmes some history of why and how the techniques were developed and who the developers were? For example, we shall see in Chapter 9 there is some dispute about how much programming Ada Lovelace did, this was only raised in the 1990's by Allen Bromley (Bromley 1990). Our knowledge of the history of this significant person should be complete.

Objections will be raised to these suggestions. Their implementation will mean that students won't have enough time to keep up to date with development: it's no use taking computing courses if students don't graduate with a knowledge of the most recent developments. But sideways radical thinking is needed. What is the use of educating only boys and men in these latest techniques if one consequence of such a policy is that women are excluded to the extent they are? This realignment of what is included is not a price to be paid for the mass inclusion of women, it is what must be done if we are to move forward.

There is further a need to develop in students a love of learning – learning cannot end when they finish their education. Technological innovation is progressing so fast that what they learn as 'current technology' may well be old by the time they reach employment. And students should be aware of the likelihood of this happening so they can factor it into their approach to further innovation. It should be clear that this is for all, for women and men, so we don't return to the situation where men think they have a right to further training and "You cannot have this because you will most probably have children". All students should enter their working life fully aware of how technology impinges on and influences gender relations.

Courses on hardware too should have history included but the purpose of including such material must be made very clear. As I query in Chapter 7: Why must we always be championing the most up-to-date equipment? Certainly, we must be aware of it, but we should also teach students the need to think analytically about robots and driverless cars. There is debate about these, but the underlying theme in the academy seems to be that students are going to learn it anyway and university courses on hardware are not the place to do it. So it is wide ranging analytical thinking that's needed as much as abstract thinking. Tutors must be able to raise moral issues and be trained in how to handle and guide the ensuing discussions.

Changes made to the computing curriculum along these lines must earn respect and be respected!

Then there is the need for more interdisciplinarity. This is complex. There is the need to ensure that not just computing but technology more generally is incorporated in the teaching of other disciplines. Teaching computing and history in parallel won't necessarily inform students of how computing has influenced history research for example. The material must be dovetailed. If this dovetailing of disciplines were started in the schools it would be less jarring to students when it continues right through their education.

There are many courses offered by UK universities combining Computer (or Computing) Science with other subjects, for example: Economic and Social History, Biology, Forensics, Geography, Business & Management, Physics. It would be interesting now to conduct research into how the two disciplines in each of these instances are made to dovetail with one another. Are, for example, ethical issues discussed at the boundaries of the disciplines, or is computer science just the same block of stuff that students were taught twenty years ago in parallel with and not impinging on the other disciplines?

The introduction of other subjects into computing courses: sociology /ethics / bias / gender/ feminism / equality and equal opportunities / history / geography / health/ biology even in a small way would give students more breadth of understanding and give them some idea of how far the implications of computing stretch. There are promising starts to these ideas, see for example *After the reboot* (Royal Society 2017, p. 43).

But there are still serious underlying problems that hinder progress. The connotations arising from the pre-existing masculine dominance are significant. Those undercurrents are still there; they are not dissipating. It seems as if those people determining how things shall move forward have not yet grasped the magnitude of their effect. Course designers continue in their belief that they know that the current ways are the correct ways of presenting the subject for maximum student take-up.

2.8 Entering the World of Paid Work

What is there to help women as they finish their education and enter the world of modern technology?

2.8.1 Women's Groups and Conferences

Internationally there are many women's tech groups whose broad objectives are to 'bring women in from the cold' but obviously they go much further than this, offering information, publishing blogs, talks, technical support and so on. They also organise conferences and the following brief survey of conferences scheduled for 2020 draws attention to some of these groups.

A search for conferences for Women in STEM for 2020 produced a full list with over 60 entries for conferences during the year (Bizzabo 2020). Most are to be held in North America with a few, less than 10, in Europe. There must be others world-wide that have not got into this list. The formats for some appear conventional, but others emphasise a variety of tech activities: hands-on and tours of labs as well as the conventional keynote speeches. Many are about leadership and self-development. Some are targeted at women interested in the business side of technology. However, it is worth noting that these discussions will not necessarily advance changes in current male-dominated leadership culture.

The most impressive feature of this list is the diversity of focus giving voice to many different groups and encouraging the intersectionality that was mentioned in the introduction; Diversity in Technology, Women of Colour, Lesbians who Tech. The diversity in many of these isn't just about the focus group but also about focussing on technical topics too: Women in Data Science and Women in Cyber Security. Some now mention STEAM (Science, Technology, Engineering, Arts and Mathematics). There is one concerned with the transformation of fashion through technology, TECH fashion week. Women of Silicon Valley and Women of Silicon Roundabout, both part of an international Women in Tech Event Series, are hosting conferences in 2020 (the latter was scheduled to be held in London). There was a WISE (Women in Science & Engineering) Conference to be held at the University of Washington and a WISE organisation in the UK.

A narrower search for conferences for Women in Computer Science produces a different but slightly overlapping selection.

BCSWomen (first set up in 1998) is part of the BCS The Chartered Institute for IT (*BCS* 2018). It offers a varied range of talks for 2018 including flexible working and collaborative working music making by the founder of the Female Laptop Orchestra, an AI Accelerator Event and listings and reports of local events around the UK. There are links for career advice.

The ACM-W group 'Supporting, celebrating and advocating for Women in Computing' (https://women.acm.org/) advertises conferences for women worldwide but, unsurprisingly given its base, by and large it doesn't show the diversity of the STEM collection either in its focus for attendees or topics. There is also the Grace Hopper Conference which was founded in 1994.

There are numerous papers delivered at these academic conferences and books describing in-depth research into women's

experiences working in technological firms. It's by no means clear just how much of this research permeates through to industrial practice. Students should surely learn of the existence of all this research so they can help ensure that it does carry through into their working environments.

On the explicitly STEM and STEAM front there are encouraging signs of activity and innovation particularly in the US. But there still remains an underlying and worrying problem that these organisations have not yet really woken up to the necessity for changing the culture. Some have been around for some years now and they are still addressing the already converted.

2.9 Other World Movements for Girls and Women

World movements rise and fall. Currently The Girl Geek Academy (https://girlgeek.io) is a movement operating mainly in the US. This one has seemingly been going since 2008:

> 'CONNECTING AND INSPIRING WOMEN IN TECH' and 'Hosting 250+ events over the past decade, Girl Geek X has created connections and shined [sic] a spotlight on 1,000+ female speakers.'

There is also Stemettes (https://stemettes.org) from the British Isles. The web page for this enterprise describes it as follows:

> Stemettes is an award winning social enterprise working across the UK & Ireland and beyond to inspire and support young women into Science, Technology, Engineering and Maths careers (known collectively as STEM).

and its mission statement reads

> To inspire the next generation of females into **Science, Technology, Engineering** and **Maths (STEM)** fields by showing them the amazing women already in STEM via a series of *panel events, hackathons, exhibitions, and mentoring schemes*

This is another organisation aimed at young women. But there is a question mark against its name. The suffix ' –ette' denotes a diminutive and feminine role. Given that this organisation is aimed at young women there is a modicum of justification for this title. However, it connotes gender specificity and, although in the past used in labels such as 'usherette', to distinguish a female usher from a male usher the tendency (not that recent) towards gender neutral labels has meant that 'new words formed using it tend to be restricted to the deliberately flippant or humorous, as, for example, bimbette and punkette'. (*–ette Oxford Dictionary Definition* 2014)

2.10 A European Organisation

2.10.1 European Institute for Gender Equality (EIGE)

EIGE is an autonomous body of the EU established to promote gender equality in all areas of life; its remit includes gender mainstreaming. In 2017 they published a general report describing a Gender Equality Index and describing changes in the index between 2005 and 2015: *Two Steps Forward, One Step Back*. As the title foretells there had been only small improvements in gender equality during that period. (European Institute for Gender Equality 2017)[7]

Although this is a general report, the Institute has also produced a number of videos on gender in STEM. One in particular cites Forbes reports using data from the US from 2014 which gives depressing data. For example, between 1984 and 2014 the percentage of women with degrees in Computer Science as compared with men fell from 37% to 12%, in 2014 women held 25% of all jobs in technology and computing, 82.6% of web designers were male. Although 80% of women in the industry reported that they loved their work, 45% said they were likely to leave the industry within a year. Work evaluation was gender biased according to 72% of respondents, 88% had critical reviews and there were frequent complaints of 'abrasiveness' occurring at these interviews and no such complaints from men. Seventy percent of women resisted the idea of asking for a pay rise.

The 2017 report was certainly not encouraging. A further report published in 2019 detailing the updated Gender Equality Index still talks about progress towards gender equality moving at a 'snail's pace' although in the right direction. EIGE gives information if not direct help to individuals on what progress there is within the EU, even if the EU doesn't include the UK any longer! In addition to these general reports, more specific topics on gender in STEM are discussed in videos and articles which can be located on the EIGE website (https://eige.europa.eu).

2.11 Where Does all this Leave Women?

Many women end their education and enter the world of paid work with high hopes that things are going to be different for them. And why shouldn't they? The book *Brotopia* (Chang 2018) which is quoted in Chapter 9 vividly demonstrates how much has gone wrong for women working in Silicon Valley and hopefully it will act as a wake-up call for new women entering the technical world of work.

The topics covered in the chapters that follow are varied, which is not surprising given the complexity of this situation, but I hope they will give encouragement, food for thought and ideas about how women can plan and run their lives in the hugely exciting world of technology.

PART II
THE FOUNDATIONS

CHAPTER 3

WHERE IS THE SCIENCE
IN COMPUTER SCIENCE?

This paper was presented in 2000 at the Women, Work and Computerization Conference held in Vancouver (WWC2000)

Abstract

THIS CHAPTER CHALLENGES THE labelling of computing as a 'science' as in 'computer science'. The reasons for labelling it in this way are political rather than intellectual, namely to keep computing in a predominantly male domain. Traditionally science involves a cluster of ideas which I call *objectivism*. Objectivism includes the idea that there are objects 'out there' for scientists to study; in computing there are none of these — they are all man made. Secondly, objectivism claims that we must not allow scientific work to be influenced by emotion – men are unemotional, women are emotional and therefore men can do science, women cannot. Women's exclusion from science for this reason has been a consistent feature since Plato, running on through the alchemists and the experimental scientists. In the same vein, by labelling computing a 'science' this myth of men's unemotionality and women's emotionality is perpetuated. The idea that men are unemotional is a myth, as evidenced by their use of highly emotional words like 'thrash', 'degrade', 'kill', 'violation' and so on.[8] The third element of objectivism is the linear development of science; science develops according to its own internal logic encapsulating some ideas, discarding others. There is an apparent linear development in computing; but this is another myth. Finally there is the distinction between pure and applied science. Pure science has more kudos than applied science and men have constructed a hierarchy with them doing the pure stuff, relegating the applied to women. I suggest the word interactionism to describe alternative ways of working which allow for pluralism and the dissolution of the hierarchies in computing.

3.1 Is Computing Really a Science?

It is no revelation that there has always been, and still is, a great deal of confusion about the identity of computing, what sort of subject it is. Though it is a new subject, people have tried to locate it in different traditional disciplines. Some would point out that historically the origins of computing lie in mathematics rather than science.

Mathematics has indeed played a significant and far-reaching role in its development. Mathematicians such as Ada Lovelace, Alan Turing and John von Neumann made critical contributions to computing as we now know it. There are some important areas of computing which are firmly based in mathematics, for example the theory of computing and formal methods. In some universities computing departments were founded from within mathematics departments and faculties. Indeed, there are those who would wish to locate computing not just within mathematics, but beyond it in new mathematics. Edsger Dijkstra in his controversial article 'On the Cruelty of Really Teaching Computer Science' in 1989 advocated the use of formal mathematics (or formal methods) as a basis for teaching computing to new students. (Dijkstra 1989)

When computing started to be taught in universities in the late 1960s and early 1970s, while some of the new departments remained closely allied to mathematics, in other institutions in the English speaking world departments of 'computer science' and 'computing science' started to appear. I work in a department of computer science as do many of my colleagues; our students are awarded degrees in computer science. The emergence of these new departments happened alongside a change in attitude to programming techniques and languages. As these developed in sophistication, men wanted to make sure that this newly emerging discipline was a male one.

In fact the discipline was, and still is, searching for an identity. Some of my colleagues talk of being computer engineers and many branches of computing have also acquired the word 'engineering' in their title. Are we discussing a discipline based on mathematics, a science discipline or an engineering discipline? Or perhaps it is none of these.

Or perhaps it is all three. As long ago as 1989 some apparent clarification of these anomalies was provided in a report written for the professional association in the US, the ACM, (Denning et al. 1989) which presented an intellectual framework for the discipline of computing. The authors used the phrase 'discipline of computing' to embrace computer science and computer engineering. There are, they say, three paradigms for the discipline. First, theory which is 'rooted in mathematics'; secondly, abstraction, which is 'rooted in the experimental scientific method' and thirdly, design, which is 'rooted in engineering'. They concluded that

> no fundamental difference exists between [computer science and computer engineering] in the core material. The differences are manifested in the way the two disciplines elaborate the core: computer science focuses on [theory] and abstraction; computer engineering on abstraction and design.

We are concerned here primarily with the supposedly scientific roots of computing. So leaving the mathematics and engineering on one side, I want to look at the parallels the authors of this report draw between the experimental scientific method and the second of their paradigms: abstraction. They list the traditional steps in scientific investigation:

1. Form a hypothesis
2. Construct a model and make a prediction
3. Design an experiment and collect data
4. Analyse results

and then go on to say "A scientist expects to iterate these steps (e.g. when a model's predictions disagree with experimental evidence)" (Denning et al. 1989, p. 10). But that is all. At no point do they draw satisfactory parallels between the natural sciences and computing. In these sciences it is aspects of the world that are being studied and the scientist tries to predict and explain these phenomena on the basis of evidence gathered either experimentally or, in the case of disciplines like astronomy, to a large extent observationally. A chemist studies chemical reactions and the biologist analyses the nature of life forms. In all these the 'scientific method' is used to understand things that exist independently of the discipline. So, what is the subject matter of so-called 'computer science'? As I shall argue in a moment, this subject matter is self-referential and concerned with man-made phenomena arising within the subject itself, rather than phenomena existing independently of the discipline.

This, it seems to me, is what underlies an interesting comment by Raj Reddy, in his acceptance lecture for the 1994 Turing award. In this lecture he recounts what Artificial Intelligence (AI) has achieved and what it could achieve in the future. In a brief discussion of the scientific method in AI he tells how "At an NRC study group meeting, a physicist asked, 'Where is the science in computer science?' 'I am happy to say' replies Reddy 'that we are beginning to have examples of the 'hypothesis, experiment, validation, and replication' paradigm within some AI systems'." (Reddy 1996, p. 109)

By that time, 1994, the discipline had been labelled a science for more than three decades. It was an extraordinary admission to say that it had taken all that time for it to acquire even a veneer of science, for it to look even superficially like a science. I say 'veneer' because even in the case of AI what these hypotheses and experiments are doing is, for instance, getting machines to recognise hand-writing and voice; they are not telling us more about speech or patterns of hand-writing.

In general, hypotheses and experiments in computing are about man-made phenomena and not the study of natural phenomena. Frederick Brooks in casting considerable doubt on the validity of and the justification for the label 'science' in the context of computer science, argues that computing produces tools not scientific truths. We test these tools by their usefulness and costs, not their novelty.

> . . . sciences legitimately take the discovery of new facts and laws as a proper end in . . . itself. A new fact, a new law is an accomplishment, worthy of publication. If we confuse ourselves with scientists, we come to take the invention . . . of endless varieties of computers, algorithms, and languages as a proper end. (Brooks 1996, p. 62)

Computing is to be valued, in other words, not in terms of the knowledge it directly contributes, but in terms of the help it can give to other disciplines which do add to knowledge. It produces tools, not finished goods, means not ends. To insist that it makes a direct contribution to scientific knowledge is to mistake means for ends. It would tend to make computing self-referential.

Hypothesising how long an algorithm will take and testing that hypothesis is sharpening our computing tools not testing a scientific hypothesis which would tell us more about the actual world.

One important point I am trying to make here is that the use or non-use of terms is not forced on the computing discipline by the inherent logic of the subject. There is sometimes some plausibility in using these terms but no more plausibility than in using other terms. It is an area where there is enough room for choice and where people are not so much discovering as creating their and their subject's identities.

This idea that people are creating their subject's identity rather than discovering it is confirmed by Wolfgang Coy (Coy 1997). He describes how the word *Informatik* came to be used in Germany more akin to computer science. Coy defines the relationship between computer science as the latter term is understood in the USA. He quotes Wolfgang Giloi writing in 1969 that the two terms were almost synonymous, so it would have been possible to use the term 'informatics' in English instead of 'computer science'. But Giloi continues "the problem one had to face . . . was that in the USA there is no common and general understanding of what this discipline should be". Coy's reaction is telling.

> This non-definition shows clearly that the whole process of introducing a new discipline was not guided by a desire of precise definition. It was instead a matter of sciento-political co-operation between interested researchers who tried to establish an inner circle while excluding unwanted or presumably less important actors.

It is my contention that the characterisations of computing as a science have indeed been used to keep out 'unwanted' or 'less important' people – namely women. And I want to justify that assertion by looking particularly at the oft-mentioned claim that science is conducted objectively and without emotion.

3.2 Objectivism in Science and Computing

I have already said that there is a crucial distinction between creating a discipline on the one hand and, on the other, discovering it. Men, it seems to me, have a vested interest in convincing everyone that we are discovering the discipline of computing, not choosing what it shall be like – and then they cannot be blamed when lo and behold it 'turns out' for example that it is a 'science' or a type of 'engineering' and so part of domains traditionally dominated by men. I shall argue that they have a vested interest in promoting, however non-explicitly, a cluster of beliefs closely related to this belief that they are discovering and not creating, a cluster I would like to call *objectivism*.

What, then, is this cluster of beliefs I call objectivism and how do men benefit from people accepting these beliefs? They are that

- there are objects 'out there' and the scientist's job is to discover the truth about these objects
- these truths will not be discovered if emotions are allowed to enter the scientific process of discovery
- this process is uniquely determined by the logic of the subject and moves from one truth to a more adequate one
- pure science attracts more prestige than applied science because it focuses more on the truths about these objects 'out there', whereas applied science pays attention to what we want to use this knowledge for.

What I shall argue is that all these factors are an integral part of scientific practice in those disciplines which are conventionally thought of as natural sciences and that computing has sought to create these factors in order to justify the label 'science'.

It is the second of these concerning the influence of emotionality, on which I want to concentrate. However, I will go through them all in order dealing with the other three only briefly.

3.2.1 Objects 'Out There'

What are these objects of knowledge as far as computing is concerned? I have already suggested that computing is not a science because it neither uses experiment (as, say, physics does) nor observation (like astronomy) to discover truths about objects 'out there'. As we have seen, it tests hypotheses about itself – it tests formulae about optimisation for searching for an item of data in large volumes of ordered data, but this is verifying the mathematics. It is not finding out if these formulae are true of the world. In general computing does not seek to investigate objects of knowledge but to provide the tools for others who do so.

3.2.2 Emotion Free Science and Computing

Emotion Free Science

The truths, about these objects which exist independently of us and which scientists are to discover, are not shaped by our choices or preferences; if we are to maximise our knowledge of them it is necessary to keep our emotions out of our investigations.

Feelings distort our perceptions and, though we cannot perhaps stop ourselves having feelings, we can make sure that they do not colour the accounts we give of our scientific 'discoveries'. Hence the requirement that impersonal language be used to describe them – scientists may not use the first person in their reports, that is they must not say 'I did X', nor use emotive words. In other words, they must be objective.

This demand for objectivity may seem to be gender innocent and not biased against either gender, but it is in fact heavily weighted against the idea of women playing an equal part in science. Traditionally scientists have to be objective and to be objective involves scientific work free of emotion. But it has always been held that women are emotional by nature and only men can achieve the emotion-free rationality required in scientific work.

I have two comments to make about this. The first is that is rather naïve to believe that men are unemotional and rational in their scientific work, and do not allow any external attitudes or emotions into it. Men do not pursue science purely out of love for the truth. The desire for prestige, fame and, indeed, fortune is just as powerful a motivation. As far as the practice of not using the first person is concerned, this seems to be a rather superficial way of trying to ensure that the scientist's emotions have not affected his work. It seems as much a cloak for hiding emotions as a guarantee that they are not at work.

Perhaps some would reply to this by saying that the work may be motivated by non-scientific emotion, but the actual work itself is free of those emotions. Professor Bloggs may want his Nobel prize, but he leaves that desire behind as soon as he enters the laboratory. Again this seems to be a rather naïve view of reality. I now turn at greater length to the other half of this myth, namely that women are unable to become scientists because they are irredeemably emotional and non-rational.

Conceptions of Western science have varied over time and have been the subject of much debate and struggle. Perhaps the most sustained way in which these different views of science have been conceptualised is in their use of sexual metaphor always at the expense of women. One thing in common to all these sexual beliefs and metaphors from ancient Greece to seventeenth century Western Europe was that they were used to reflect and reinforce women's inferiority both as far as their ability to practise science is concerned and their position in the social hierarchy.

In her book *Reflections on Gender and Science* Evelyn Fox Keller (Keller 1995) examines the sexual metaphors in the scientific theories of Plato, the modern or experimental science much influenced by Francis Bacon and the science of the alchemists, or hermetic science. It is Francis Bacon and his experimental method that I wish to concentrate on eventually, but I will briefly mention both Plato and the alchemists in order to highlight the use of sexual metaphor to show the continuing struggle over the definition of science and the perpetual position of women at the bottom of the pile – men always ending up on top.

Plato, particularly in his dialogue The Symposium, had been influenced by the ideals of Athenian love. The most idealised was homosexual love between two men, the lover and the loved. While this was a hierarchical relationship in the sense that the lover was usually an adult and the one who was loved a youth, it nonetheless avoided domination. It was a union involving desire on the part of the lover but one which did not compromise the dignity of the beloved, who would himself one day become a lover. The beloved was affectionate, but dispassionate and never subjugated himself to his lover by showing desire – as for example women did in heterosexual love (Keller 1995, Chapter 1). This conception of women being subject to powerful emotional influences within themselves, particularly by showing sexual desires is one which, as we shall see, continues throughout the conceptions of science we shall touch upon and indeed right up to the present day. It has always been a way of disqualifying women from an equal place in scientific investigation.

It is difficult to summarise the extremely varied beliefs and practices of the natural magicians, alchemists and hermetic scientists. These names in fact represent different philosophies. But, very broadly speaking, they all opposed the traditional Galenic and Aristotelian views of medicine. They believed in the transformative and curative powers of chemically prepared medicine. The practice of turning base metals into gold was, according to Keller, largely emblematic, by which I assume she means that it was symbolic and not one of their major working aims.

For the Renaissance alchemists the universe was very harmonious as Giambattista della Porta wrote

> The whole world is knit and bound within itself: for the world is a living creature, everywhere both male and female, and the parts of it do couple together . . . by reason of their mutual love. (Merchant 1990, p. 104)

Although many of the alchemists were experimental and exhorted enquirers to "use their hands and not their fancies" (Vaughan 1919) when investigating Nature, Thomas Vaughan was able to exhort his fellow Paracelsians "to magic in the magician's phrase: 'hear with the understanding of the heart'" (Vaughan

1919, p. 77). The harmony and love in the world meant that for the alchemists the emphasis was on coition, or sexual union, and some of them almost speak as if the two genders were equal. Thomas Vaughan wrote "the magician's sun and moon are two universal peers, male and female, a king and queen regents . . ." (p. 94).

In spite of this the alchemists were in many ways contemptuous of women whilst, at the same time, almost reverencing their procreative powers. Indeed Thomas Vaughan also wrote that the "Soul of man consists chiefly of two Portions . . . the *superior Masculine* and *Eternall,* the *inferior Foeminine* and *Mortall."* (Vaughan 1919, p. 77) . And earlier, Paracelsus while being a champion of the poor and disadvantaged and demanding radical changes in society was, in spite of this, a misogynist.

In Francis Bacon's characterisations of science, the sort of characterisation which later came to be known as 'Experimental Science', the whole tone of the relationship between Nature and those who investigate Nature shifts strongly into the coercive half of the spectrum. Nature is, of course, seen as female and her male investigators are depicted in Bacon's metaphors as engaging in a wide range of ways of dominating her. At the less aggressive end of the spectrum he asserts that:

> . . . man is but the servant and interpreter of nature: what he does and what he knows is only what he has observed of nature's order in fact or in thought . . . For the chains of causes cannot by any force be loosed or broken, nor can nature be commanded except by being obeyed. (Bacon 1858, p. 32)

Bacon also talks of science being "A chaste and lawful marriage between Mind and Nature." (p. 36) But at the more violent end of the spectrum, science is to "conquer", "subdue" and storm "her castles and strongholds". There is also talk of torture: "nature exhibits herself more clearly under the trials and vexation of art [torture] than when left to herself" (Bacon 1858, p. 298). Carolyn Merchant suggests that Bacon's metaphors depicting torture are reminiscent of the interrogations of witches and the devices used to obtain confessions from them (p. 168). There is also, of course, rape: men can "hound nature in her wanderings" and should make no scruple of "entering and penetrating into these holes and corners, when the inquisition of truth is his whole object" (Bacon 1858, p. 296).

Nature was to be made subservient to science. Science was to dominate her just as men were to dominate women. Joseph Glanvill, later to be a Fellow of and a propagandist for the Royal Society of London, wrote in 1661

> [W]here the *Will*, or *Passion* hath the casting voyce, the case of *Truth* is desperate. ... The *Woman* in us, still prosecutes a deceit, like that begun in the *Garden*: and our *Understandings* are wedded to an *Eve*, as fatal as the *Mother* of our *miseries*. (Glanvill 1661, p. 71).

As always, women are seen as a danger to the pursuit of truth and science. Experimentation to test hypotheses is crucial to Bacon's conception of science. Yet, interestingly, I am not aware of any experiment on Bacon's part to establish the inferiority of women as scientists or in general. Neither Bacon's audience nor any other audience at that time demanded evidence of this; it seemed to them self-evident.

In 1664 Henry Oldenburg, the Secretary to the Royal Society, wrote in a preface (entitled *The Publisher to the Reader*) to a book by Robert Boyle that it was the intention of the Society to "raise a Masculine Philosophy whereby the Mind of Man may be enobled with the Knowledge of solid Truths, and the Life of Man benefited with ampler accommodations, than it hath been hitherto." (Boyle 1664)

These seventeenth century philosophers had become preoccupied with the dangerous female sex. These views of science were those of a masculine activity enmeshed in a male dominated society. The mechanical philosophy of Descartes upgraded masculine procreativity, God the Father had created the world by himself and without female assistance (Easlea 1980); God was male, Man ruled the Universe, Man controlled Nature and, above all, men controlled and dominated women. Keller remarks that Nature is indubitably female and the object of men's actions (Keller 1995, p. 39) – henceforth men are more and more able to do what they want with her.

It seems as if keeping women out was important in all of these philosophies and in the case of Baconian science as important as experimentation. Indeed, in the case of Bacon whatever experimentation might reveal, it was already quite clear that women were not fit to engage in science. All these philosophies have greatly influenced the development of and attitudes to modern science. How does its genesis and continuing existence affect us now? More particularly, how does it affect computing?

It is against this traditional background of casting women in the role of emotion-driven people that the demand for objectivity is to be seen. Women are, in effect, debarred from scientific activity by this persistent characterisation of them as emotional beings. But this half of the myth is more what men have wanted to believe than what is true.

We have already seen that the other half of the myth, namely that men are unemotional in the pursuit of science, is what they would like to believe and is as far from the truth as their assertions about women. (It is interesting that Bacon can envisage men as wanting to rape and pillage but does not want to see any emotional content in those desires.)

Emotion Free Computing

In the case of computing, not only is emotive language frequently used, it is also consistently indicative of deeply underlying male attitudes. The subject is peppered with words like 'thrash', 'violation', 'degrade', not to mention the often quoted 'kill', 'abort', 'execute' and less constantly used 'squirting data'? Surely such a vocabulary rich in violence, aggression, domination, male potency and so on gives the lie to the other half of the myth that men are rational and unemotional. Men are very far indeed, as this vocabulary shows, from being unemotional.

There appears to be very little remaining of the myth once it is examined, but of course those who deny that there is such a myth are unlikely to examine it. As Keller points out:

> Unexamined myths wherever they survive, have a subterranean potency; they affect our thinking in ways we are not aware of, and to the extent that we lack awareness, our capacity to resist their influence is undermined (Keller 1995, p. 76).

That the old myth is still alive and well is beautifully illustrated by the reaction of one of my senior colleagues to my list of Baconian metaphors. He said "Can't you find anything more up-to-date than that?" implying that these metaphors belonged way back in the history of science, when only two days before he had himself been threatening to get academic papers from us by "coming around with forceps if necessary".

3.2.3 Linear Development

Linear Development in Science

The third item in this cluster I have called objectivism is the belief that science is developing along uniquely determined lines and according to its own internal logic. This means that a given scientific discipline has to be what it is at any given point in time. There is no choice in this. As science develops over time some ideas are discarded; others, on the other hand, become encapsulated in theories with an increasing range of explanatory power.

A prime example of this linear development is Astronomy. Copernicus challenged the geocentric systems of Aristotle and

Ptolemy which eventually were agreed to be false and discarded; he, Copernicus, devised a system in which the earth orbits the sun with other planets. Kepler, while reinforcing much of Copernican theory, also discovered that planetary motion is elliptical and not circular. Galileo too strengthened Copernican theory, although his greater contribution was to mechanics. Later, Newton used the work of Kepler, Galileo and others to develop his own comprehensive physics which can be used to explain the movement of heavenly bodies. (Chalmers 1999)

Linear Development in Computing

In computing too this linear development seems to occur in, for example, AI (Whitby 1996, pp. 20–24) and in database management systems. In fact, older systems are often abandoned, not because they have been intellectually discredited and shown to be false, but for economic reasons. While men may not actually say that the outmoded systems are false, they certainly behave as if they are. In fact, there is scope for considerable pluralism here, at any rate if one forgets the economics for a moment and concentrates on the intellectual side. Pluralism suggests several ways of doing the same thing and in a situation like that there is little opportunity for anyone to lay down the law about the correct way of doing things.

On the other hand, everyone expects a science to be making linear progress whereby yesterday's truth, if not disproved, is nevertheless overtaken by today's new discoveries. And here there is much more scope for telling people what to do and a need for a hierarchy by means of which they are told how they should do things. By labelling computing a 'science' one blocks the non-hierarchical implications of pluralism. I think I detect in all this a hint of men making out of 'computer science' what they want it to be – a pretext for their authoritarianism.

3.2.4 Pure and Applied

Pure and Applied Science

The final part of the package of ideas imported into computing by calling it a 'science' is the distinction between 'pure' and 'applied' science. Pure science attracts more prestige than applied science because, in it, the object of study (the cell, the atom or the planet) is insulated from the factors outside science which dictate the objectives of applied sciences, for example, our wish to produce more attractive medicines or sources of energy. The engineer who has to apply laws of physics and mechanics is less highly regarded than the person who discovers these laws.

There may even be instances of this difference in status levels within pure science. Sharon Traweek in her book *Beamtimes and Lifetimes* describes how in institutions for research into high energy physics she saw few experimentalists in the offices of theorists and how several theorists told her that "an experimentalist would probably feel very awkward amongst the theorists, who have more status." (Traweek 1988, p. 33)

Pure and Applied Computing

This is true in computing too. The academic or the industrial researcher who develops new ideas and makes new computing tools for others to use, is more highly regarded than those who use the tools.

If one were to draw a kind of map of computing and its personnel (see Figure 3.1) which depicts the way that the practitioners see it, there is in both the workplace and academic computing a central core of 'pure' computing untainted by the 'mess' of people and everyday circumstances. At this centre we have an elite, largely male. In the map this is the inner circle of these concentric circles. This central elite makes the 'discoveries' and hands out the truths about these discoveries to the outer circles. As one moves into these outer circles and into the 'messy' areas away from the pure central area where the 'discoveries' are made, one moves into the areas where these 'discoveries' are applied. At the same time the importance of computing and the kudos awarded to those doing it diminishes and the number of women involved rises correspondingly. The further out the ring is from the pure centre the lower the prestige and the higher the proportion of women. In the outer rings one is merely applying the truths that those in the inner ring have gained, or in my view, created.

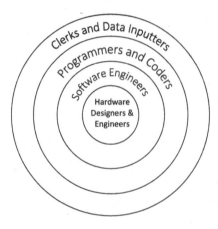

Figure 3.1: *Relationships between computing personnel*

The outer rings of this computing map are those which involve more interaction with people. And indeed this map illustrates what was the accepted wisdom in the early days of computing. The attitude was that the more pure and abstract computing remained the better. Those discussions with end-users which did take place were more in the nature of authoritative handing-down of truths. This early approach of 'handing down' a computing system may have now largely disappeared in some countries and other pockets where it has been replaced by a more sensitive and involved approach towards the end-user, but its influence still remains strong.

In labelling computing as a science men in this way have introduced this myth of objectivism with its ideas of the absence of emotion, linear progression and pure and applied science to justify hierarchy, power, authoritarianism and degrees of kudos.

3.3 Interactionism

Finally, I outline the sort of positive alternative I would like to propose in the light of my criticisms of objectivism. This alternative I have labelled interactionism. Just as objectivism is a cluster of ideas so too is interactionism.

Let me start with the rejection of the idea of a linear progression in computing and the assumption that yesterday's belief is 'false'. As soon as one rejects this, pluralism immediately becomes possible, there would be a plurality of alternative ways of tackling a problem from which one could choose what suited the situation and also suited oneself and what one felt 'at home' with. It is not a matter of simply accepting some objective 'truth', whether one likes it or not. Because of the pluralism and because there is no one correct way of doing things, there would be far less tendency to refer decisions to some higher layer of a hierarchy or to some inner ring. This, amongst other things, would greatly encourage co-operative working at the periphery – except that the periphery wouldn't be there any longer, the idea of some centre with a body of pure truths which are applied at the periphery would have gone and with it much of the elitism and hierarchy which are so valued by the men. Many people would be newly empowered by such a dissolution of authority.

This, amongst other things, would greatly encourage co-operative working at the periphery as already occurs to a certain extent in CSCW. The final contrast between the old objectivism and this new interactionism is that interactionism will involve a blurring of the distinction between subject and object. A good example of this is role playing and the new personae that can achieved by playing in Multi-User Domains (or MUD's).

Just as in the co-operative writing of fiction there is no distinction between reader and writer so I am suggesting that the same dynamic could occur in the creation of software. You will not be discovering something 'out there', you will be taking part in the creation of it. For this democratisation and the parallel disappearance of the centres of excellence to take place there is of course a need for high levels of computer literacy. Then there is no limit, in principle, to those who could be enfranchised in this democracy.

This conception of interactionism differs from interaction as it is generally understood in computing circles where a distinction is made between algorithms and interaction. (See for example (Wegner 1997).) Computationally, algorithmic and interactive systems may be different, but in terms of my interactionism they are not. Interactionism places more emphasis on human intervention with the software, and the complexity of the input humans provide implies more indeterminacy in the outcome. It is difficult to illustrate what I have in mind with traditional examples like smart bombs, banking systems and so on, because they require a very specific outcome so not to be able to show that that outcome will be the result, implies failure.

We should be looking beyond these traditional applications from the world of computing to applications like the example above of co-operative writing of software for a better understanding of what interactionism implies. We are far too busy travelling along the same railway track set out for us by computer scientists who seem determined to keep the discipline on that straight and narrow path that they would like to convince us is self-determining.

CHAPTER 4

COMPUTER ENGINEERING: ENGINEERING WHAT?

This paper was first published in AISB Quarterly, Issue 100, pp. 24–31, 1998

Abstract

THERE IS CURRENTLY A shift in computing to an engineering paradigm. In this chapter I challenge the justification for using the word 'engineering' at all in the context of computing. Computing has adopted this word to refer not just to hardware but to software as well. Software engineers talk of designing and constructing software, but to use the word 'construct' in this context is already to tilt the listener towards the world of masculine dominated engineering. Along with the label 'engineering' come all sorts of other factors: words like 'engine' and 'tools', the brotherhood of professional associations, humour directed against women and minorities and a traditional contempt for 'soft' subjects like sociology. There is too the eroticism that is so often intertwined with engineering, as in James Bond films for example. There are two types of division in engineering; a stratification between different types of engineering and the straightforward exclusion of women from all types. As far as the recruitment of women entering computing is concerned there is a danger that the shift from a mathematics to an engineering paradigm will deter even more women than have been deterred already.

4.1 The Motivation for this Chapter

In the academic world computing is often labelled 'computer science' or 'computing science'. I have questioned above in Chapter 3 the use of the label 'science' to describe the subject. The gist of this criticism is that computing in no way attempts to explain natural phenomena as traditional experimental science does. This can be seen by focusing on its subject matter rather than on its methodology. All sciences have a subject matter and one is entitled to ask what things any science deals with. For instance, a child might ask what seismology is about and be told it is the scientific study of earthquakes. If we ask in this way what the subject matter of computer science is, the answer could not be it is the study of computers, if one means by 'computers' simply assemblages of things like metal and plastic. Not only can computers not be understood without reference to software and programming, they clearly cannot be understood unless recognised as machines deliberately designed to do certain jobs. They can only be understood with reference to the human purposes for which they have been designed and built. Any link between science and computing must be the *application of various sciences* to the ongoing project of designing better and better machinery cum software to do the ever-expanding jobs we now realise computers can be designed to do.

Hypotheses and experiments in computing are about man-made phenomena and not the study of natural phenomena. Frederick Brooks in casting considerable doubt on the validity of and the justification for the label 'science' in the context of computer science argues that computing produces tools not scientific truths. We test these tools by their usefulness and costs, not their novelty.

> ... sciences legitimately take the discovery of new
> facts and laws as a proper end in itself. A new
> fact, a new law is an accomplishment, worthy of
> publication. If we confuse ourselves with scientists,
> we come to take the invention ... of endless varieties
> of computers, algorithms, and languages as a proper
> end. (Brooks 1996, p. 62)

Computing is to be valued, in other words, not in terms of the knowledge it directly contributes, but in terms of the help it can give to other disciplines which do add to knowledge. It produces tools, not finished goods, means not ends. The kind of experiment undertaken in computing is not about 'the world' but a matter of testing hypotheses about computing procedures themselves. These hypotheses and experiments are self-referential. As an early experimentalist like Francis Bacon might well have observed "You can't make a science out of navel gazing!"

There are no scientific laws of computing any more than there are laws discovered by a science called motorcarology, although of course, more and more science of materials, mechanics, electronics and so on can be used in providing an ever improving method of personal transport. In the same way discoveries from other areas can be fed into computing, an applied science in which knowledge gained in other sciences, e.g. electronics, is used to achieve a particular result. In this respect, in fact, it is more like engineering (or, perhaps, applied science) than it is like a natural science.

The use of the label 'science' in this context of computing is quite gratuitous; and one is forced to look for reasons other than intellectually constraining features of computing for an explanation of the widespread use of the term 'computer science'. The label has been used to hitch this new subject to the ever-rising star of science and thereby share in the kudos it enjoys. I also believe it is used to assert male dominance of the discipline in a way parallel to that in which this same dominance has been asserted in and through all scientific philosophies from Plato onwards.

When challenged about this, some computer scientists tend nowadays to concur with the criticism that computing is not a science and respond by saying that the subject is more akin to engineering than to science. The word is now well established in computing, not only for the discipline as a whole as in 'computer engineering', but also for topics within it – topics such as software engineering, data engineering and knowledge engineering. I now look briefly at the evolution of engineering and the motivations for and the consequences of the use of this word in the world of computing and, of course, the consequences for women.

4.2 The Origins of 'Engineering'

The early meaning of the word 'engineer' was one 'who designs and constructs military engines [e.g. siege catapults] or works'. It also came to mean 'one who designs and constructs works of public utility'. From the 18th century such a person was also called a 'civil engineer' originally distinguishing him from a military engineer although the distinction later was between civil engineering and mechanical engineering. (*engineer | Shorter Oxford English Dictionary* 1979) We now, of course, have other engineers of all sorts: electrical, electronic, marine, chemical, agricultural and so on. In the past engineering was not based so much on a formal application of science and mathematics as on informal know-how based on experience and embodied in knowledge that was often passed from father to son – or in the case of Sally Hacker – father to daughter (Hacker 1990). A more modern definition of engineering is "The application of science and mathematics by which the properties of matter and the sources of energy in nature are made useful to people." (*engineering | Merriam-Webster Dictionary* 2018) implying more formal use of scientific experimentation – hence the notion of 'applied science'.

The dominant picture that the word 'engineering' evokes is of somebody realigning matter (e.g. metal and concrete) and physical forces (e.g. gravity and electricity) to achieve a desired physical end, a bridge that stands up or an engine that works. Engineers typically produce artefacts. And the world of engineering in all these fields implies masculinity; the word 'engineer' evokes the image of a man.

Two more recent additions concern living things: genetic and social engineering. Genetic engineering by no means implies large artefacts, but it does imply intervention and the strong possibility of control. Social engineering implies intervening in society and realigning existing societal forces to bring about changes which would not otherwise occur. Social engineering differs from the other types of engineering I have just mentioned in that it is not a profession; the term 'social engineering' is used only to describe a practice and, for some people, this practice has sinister overtones.

In parallel with this last meaning we also now have a more general use which appears in the phrase 'engineering a situation' by which we mean bringing it about and having some effect on the world by making an intervention in the world as we find it. Webster's Dictionary also defines engineering as 'skilful or artful contrivance or manipulation'. All these newer meanings reflect the interventionist nature of engineering. The widespread use of these newer meanings of the word does nothing to detract from its masculinity.

4.3 Computing's Adoption of the Word 'Engineering'

In this section I examine some of the possible motivations for computing's adoption of the word 'engineering' particularly in the context of software engineering.

4.3.1 Computer Hardware and Engineering

Computer hardware is a technological artefact. Its design and construction require the skills of electronic engineers who are 'manipulating matter and realigning forces'. And we need engineers in the traditional sense of the word to maintain these machines.

So, the word as used in this earlier sense is quite applicable and appropriate when applied to these activities of building and maintaining computers.

However, for a long time now the line between hardware and software has been a shifting one. It became cheaper and more efficient to 'hard code' or 'hard wire' many functions rather than write software code to achieve them. So there is a shifting, wiggly line between what is hardware and what is software. This is certainly one factor which may have contributed to the idea that programming could be an engineering discipline.

4.3.2 Computer Software and Engineering

What I wish to discuss in this paper is the transfer of this word from hardware to software. 'Engineering' is now widely used to describe the design, construction and maintenance of software. Computing has adopted the word 'engineering' to describe a number of different sub-disciplines under the overarching discipline of computing. An ACM report of 1989 defines the discipline of computing as embracing both computer science and computer engineering (so in fact the label 'science' has by no means been abandoned, both are still current). According to this ACM report there are three paradigms underlying the discipline: theory, rooted in mathematics; abstraction, rooted in the scientific method; and design, rooted in engineering. Computer science is based on the first two paradigms and computer engineering on the latter two. (Denning et al. 1989, p. 10)

The paradigm for abstraction consists of the traditional steps of scientific investigation:

1. Form a hypothesis
2. Construct a model and make a prediction
3. Design an experiment and collect data
4. Analyse results

As I have already argued, the hypotheses and predictions involved are internal to computing, part of its own attempts to produce packages of machines and software which will do more and more for us. In other words, computing is much more like the design paradigm rooted in engineering described by Denning et al. as consisting of four steps needed for the construction of a system (or device) to solve a given problem

1. state requirements
2. state specifications
3. design and implement the system
4. test the system (p. 10)

Computer engineering in this context is concerned primarily with software and many of the practitioners call themselves software engineers. The term 'software engineering' was first used at a conference held in Munich in 1968; the profession of software engineer is now widely accepted.

But how justified is the use of this term? What I shall argue is that on all sides meanings of words are stretched, masculine terms are used and restrictive practices are adopted in order to ensure that this subject is defined in terms of a male domain.

Proponents of the use of the word 'engineering' say this kind of engineering is about the synthesis of different disciplines, and it is about building and therefore it is engineering. And many software engineers justify their title with the argument that they are designing, constructing and testing software just as civil engineers, for example, construct bridges. Typical of this way of thinking is the view expressed by (Parnas 1997) that the fact that 'bridges, engines, aircraft and power plants', which require engineers to build them, are designed and controlled by software justifies calling the process of writing the software 'engineering'. Or again as GFC Rogers writes

That software engineering is an engineering discipline is a simple consequence of the fact that 'engineering refers to the practice of organising the design and construction of an artifice which transforms the physical world around us to meet some recognised need' (Rogers 1983, p. 51)

There are certainly parallels here. The difference is that civil engineers are making use of tangible materials like steel and concrete and forces like gravity and electricity whereas software engineers do not produce 'things' at all. To describe software as an artifice, or as an artefact, is stretching the meaning of that word in order to be able to bring computing into the world of engineering. Software seems to be much more like a recipe for making a cake than the cake, a real thing, which results from following it.

Supporters of the word 'engineering' will then defend themselves by saying that they fashion collections of software to make 'tools' used in the design and construction of bridges and so on. But these are not physical artefacts like hammers and spanners, they are tools only in a metaphorical sense. And of course, what metaphors we use are not forced on us. They are a matter of our choice. It is interesting to note that 'tools' is suggestive of masculine pursuits (just as the phrase 'constructing software' is already) to tilt and guide the listener towards thinking of masculine industries as in constructing buildings, aircraft and ships – all of which produce large, dominating artefacts which computer software manifestly does not. The use of all this vocabulary, 'engineering', 'tools', 'constructing', seems to be an attempt to assimilate the writing of software to the male domain.

One way in which software designers seem to be emulating the practices of colleagues in the more established engineering disciplines is in using mathematical or formal methods for checking their designs at an early stage. In his article 'Software's Chronic Crisis' (Gibbs 1994) mentions a number of software failures where mathematical tests were not used or were not reliable. He quotes the chairman of one software company as saying

> . . . engineers rely on mathematical analysis to predict how their designs will behave in the real world. Unfortunately, the mathematics that describes physical systems does not apply within the synthetic binary universe of a computer program; discrete mathematics, a far less mature field, governs here. But using the still limited tools of set theory and predicate calculus, computer scientists have contrived ways to translate specifications and programs into the language of mathematics . . . (p. 7)

The contriving of some 'computer engineers' may appear clever to those who wish to ensure the continuation of the engineering paradigm, but to others it appears to be a contrivance which is unconvincing. Maibaum is convinced of the engineering parallel and, in consequence, is concerned to advocate curricula for software engineering which reflect engineering principles. (Maibaum 1997)

> I firmly believe software engineering *could* reflect engineering principles . . . We could populate a software engineering curriculum with material reflecting this appropriate foundational material . . . in spite of the . . . immaturity of the subject and the underlying computer science. It is simply a matter of will for software engineering academics and software engineering practitioners [to] recognise the importance and applicability of engineering principles in the construction of software artefacts. (p. 41)

But his students do not seem to share his faith in this paradigm. He teaches 3rd year students software engineering using positive examples from science and traditional engineering and a few from software engineering (I presume by 'positive' he means successful projects) and using a multitude of negative examples from software engineering. Although some students responded constructively to the material, most students could not see the relevance of mathematical, scientific and engineering principles and practices. This response, suggests Maibaum, shows up a deficiency from the point of view of engineering, in the attitudes, concepts and skills lecturers inculcate in the students. Is he, perhaps unwittingly, admitting that computing academics don't really in fact believe in this sufficiently deeply to be able to convince their students? And is it possible that this is because this paradigm is a poor fit?

The realisation that computing is not a science is a slow process and the move to change the label from 'science' to 'engineering' is taking place within boundaries set up by men and amongst a community which is dominated by men. So the debate is taking place within the world of science and engineering and amongst scientists, engineers and mathematicians – the vast majority of whom are men. There is no debate about any other options as the label for the activity they are engaged in changes from that of one masculine activity to another – from science to engineering. As we have seen, the only debate which does take place concerns how to justify the new label.

Why do the parallels and hence the names always have to be with activities which are identified with male professions and male activities? For instance, when many other things are produced as a result of the work of software engineers, why is it that the metaphors are all taken from massive, almost exclusively male, engineering activities?

Software engineers will say that the kind of precision and care required by their profession parallels the precision needed to make sure a bridge is safe. For both software engineers and civil engineers errors can prove fatal. But this could just as easily be said about cooking. Cooking has, on occasions, to be extremely precise. And it must be safe or people may die just as surely as they will die if they are on a bridge which collapses. One reason is that cookery skills are less prominent and regarded as less important. They are less prominent thanks to the relative values patriarchal society places on these activities, but cooking is hardly less important. Another possibility is to find parallels with the stereotypical female work of caring. But this is easily dismissed because it is too 'messy'. As I have argued elsewhere (Grundy 1996, Chapter 5.1) men do the pure work which is more easily defined and women do the messy work which is less easy to plan and predict. This argument about other analogies and metaphors always leads into a vicious circle. Male activities are prestigious and prominent, female activities not so; no matter how important they are for survival. And because male activities earn more respect, they are used to provide the metaphors, and ultimately the vocabulary, for newly emerging professions. This ensures the continuation of the prestige of masculine activities which will again be used to justify the use of metaphors associated with the masculine. And so on.

4.4 What Else Comes with this Word 'Engineering'?

4.4.1 Words

In labelling computing an engineering subject men may, on the one hand, be ascribing new meanings to the word, but on the other hand they are carrying over into the new meanings attendant vocabulary which reinforces masculine dominance partly by means of all the old masculine overtones and connotations. For example, we have already noted how the word 'tools' is used to describe units of program which software engineers can use to 'build' their systems and to make other 'tools'.

Stereotypical female tasks like housework and cookery do not use 'tools'. And the word 'engine' is frequently used to describe a large piece of software, a use of the word by men which is extremely difficult to challenge. But to me they are not and never were 'engines' and I do not use the word in this context – it is too reminiscent of boys and trains and large locomotive engines which are overbearing and slightly threatening as they draw into the station as I wait on the platform.

4.4.2 Brotherhoods

Not only are words being carried over to underpin the masculinity of this new activity, but they are reproducing the social networks of engineering, the brotherhood. There is, first, the social brotherhood and the bonding that is assisted by the presence of the hardware and software and the consequent near absence of women. Secondly there is the brotherhood provided by membership of the professional associations. In the case of computing and software engineering in particular these have been modelled on the old engineering professional associations (Parnas 1997). Using these existing engineering, and thus predominantly male, institutions as models is another way in which the masculinity of engineering is being brought into computer engineering (see also (Vehviläinen 1997)). These professional associations are set up to guarantee the qualifications and standards of work of members. But they also serve another important function, the existence of societies dominated and run by men which play a large part in determining how the profession will develop.

With the socialising amongst the brotherhood comes the humour. This is also present in the classroom where, as Sally Hacker points out, "Professors' jokes transmit values warning the students what to avoid and what to emulate". Hacker reports scatological (which, roughly speaking, means lavatorial) jokes in the engineering classroom. I have seen 'jokes' circulated by students in the computing laboratory in which the classes ridiculed are women and minorities. I am not saying that these came directly from professors. What I am suggesting is that the male environment, which includes something conferred on it by the presence of computing equipment and near absence of women, encourages the use of this type of humour. Both these types of humour, scatological and sexual, denigrate the body and thereby raise the status of the abstract and the mechanical. (Hacker 1990, pp. 118–121).

These values include not just humour used for the direct denigration of women but also for denigrating those intellectual activities in which women predominate. "Scientists and engineers stand on the shoulders of giants. Social scientists stand on their faces" (Hacker 1990, p. 119). It has been suggested to me many times that the work I do, as manifest in this paper and other publications, is sociology. This is emphatically not the case. What I am engaged in is research into computing. By labelling what I do as sociology, not only can my work be ignored because it belongs to another discipline and is therefore not real computing, but it can also be dismissed as 'soft' and thus unworthy of serious consideration.

4.4.3 Male Reproduction

We have just seen how, in engineering and computing, humour is used to place the body in an inferior position to the abstract and mechanical. This is parallel to the distinction and division between mind and body. Masculine pursuits require abstract and theoretical skills while female pursuits require the body and practical thinking. But this pursuit of the technical without women leaves men still with a desire to show that they can reproduce. Sally Hacker reports how Lewis Mumford

> . . . traces the 'deity that presided over the new religion and the new mechanical world picture' of the sixteenth and seventeenth centuries to the ancient 'Atum-Re, the self created Sun, who out of his own semen had created the universe and all the subordinate deities . . . without the aid of the female principle. (Hacker 1990, p. 122)

Engineering, particularly military engineering, allows men to simulate reproduction without women. Brian Easlea in *Fathering the Unthinkable* (Easlea 1987) describes how the atom bombs which were tested at Los Alamos at the end of the second world war were referred to as 'babies'. When a test was successful it was a male birth and coded messages announced 'It's a boy' and when it was unsuccessful it was a female birth and signalled with the message 'It's a girl'. How can anyone deny the continuity of thought underlying these things when these phrases are so reminiscent of Francis Bacon's desire for the development of science which he likened to a 'masculine birth'? (Keller 1985, p39)

In computing too we have hardware engineers simulating birth without female intervention. A small scale experimental machine, the first stored-program computer, was called 'the Baby' by those who built it in Manchester, England in 1948. The Baby was rebuilt, by different people but with some parts, valves for example, manufactured around the time, to mark the 50th anniversary of its 'birth'. And there was to be an 'Official Birthday Party' in June 1998. (50th Anniversary Celebrations 1997). It is perhaps reassuring to these engineers that they can still achieve the simulated procreation that their predecessors did.

Throughout the history of computing the hardware has always been built by members of a male engineering profession (and in the rebuilding of 'Baby', with all its attendant publicity, they are making sure we don't forget it). Men eventually appropriated the production of the software once they realised how important they could make it and have been trying to establish an identity and a profession for this type of work ever since. The proximity of the hardware to the software and the obvious need for hardware has provided one excuse for identifying software with engineering.

4.4.4 Engineering and Eroticism

Sally Hacker argues that just as reason and passion were once fused so too were technology and eroticism. She cites other authors who describe the life centred bio-technics of the Neolithic age where technology and eroticism were one set of activities. Gardens, for example, were both essential for life and the source of sensual pleasure in food and perfume. Social technologies were as important as tool technology. It was an age of egalitarianism not of matriarchy. Later this changed. The first great engineering feats, the pyramids, were accomplished by patriarchal, hierarchically organised societies. And at that point technology and eroticism were deemed separate spheres. But in spite of or perhaps because of the split, technology and eroticism are still closely intertwined and Hacker gives plenty of examples in the field of engineering.

For example, she quotes Samuel C. Florman (Florman 1996):

> McKenna's description of engineer meeting engine "Hello engine. I'm Jake Holman" he said under his breath. Jake Holman loved machinery in the way some other men love God, women and their country. (Hacker 1990, p. 208)

Carol Cohn, a college teacher, describes in an article how she learnt about nuclear weapons in a summer workshop given by some of the most distinguished experts in the field. Sexual imagery was rife and there was no attempt to hide it ". . . lectures were concerned with discussion of vertical erector launchers, thrust-to-weight ratios, soft lay downs, deep penetration, and the comparative advantages of protracted versus spasm attacks" (Cohn 1996, p. 174). But, she continues later, their techno-jargon with phrases such as 'collateral damage' (which is another way of saying 'mass murder') provides a smooth, shiny surface under which there exist "strong currents of homoerotic excitement, heterosexual domination . . ." (p. 183). James Bond stories and films with their sexy women and scarcely credible technology emphasise both the erotic and the technical and illustrate nicely how the technical feeds the erotic and vice versa. And computers are still widely advertised using voluptuous women as an integral part of the advertising technique (Lander & Adam 1997). But concentrating on this masks the important point that all this is for control – the control of women.

Here is another example of the intertwining of the erotic with another male dominated subject, mathematics, which demonstrates just how close they can be in the eyes of men. In a mathematics book entitled *Groupes Stables* in which the text is entirely about group theory, the author has interleaved in his text pictures of naked women (Poizat 1987). At the end there is a photograph of the author in his dressing gown. What function do these photographs serve in a book in which there is not one single reference to them? They are there to entertain male readers and if they do entertain some female readers it is on a quite different basis to the way in which male readers are entertained. They are there to demonstrate to young female readers that their role is to be objectified; they are there to indicate to older female readers that they no longer have a role to play; they are there to place men, particularly mathematicians, above women in the social hierarchy. But the placement between pages of mathematical formulae also shows how mathematics and the erotic are intertwined and that for some people mathematics possibly does have emotional and/or erotic power. But that erotic power is being used in this case to relegate women to the position of the 'other'. It is impossible to illustrate what the situation would be if we reversed the roles of men and women in this kind of situation. We do not have the imagery, the words or the political power to show men in the truly equivalent position of those women in that mathematics text book.

Sally Hacker quotes Tracy Kidder's book, *The Soul of a New Machine* (Kidder 2011) which describes the circumstances surrounding the building of a new computer in the 1970s, as an example of the intensity of the relationship between man and machine. The building of the machine is a process in which man is gaining control of the machine; this is a substitute for reciprocal relationships. And there's plenty more of that in *Hackers* (Levy 1984) a book about programming from the early sixties onwards.

Ellen Ullman in her book *Close to the Machine* in which she describes her experiences as a software engineer writes "We give ourselves over to . . . the nearly sexual pleasure of the clicking thought stream" (Ullman 1997, p. 15). One wonders if modern technology does not have the same pull for those computer engineers of today engaged in the recreation of the Baby in Manchester. Is their enthusiasm for rebuilding to recreate some of the eroticism that surrounded the building of the first 'Baby'? And is the move to an engineering paradigm within computing an attempt to bring back that eroticism? (Again, like the aggressive language of 'execute', 'abort', 'kill' and so on, this hardly fits with the official view that the discipline is objective and its practitioners leave their emotions outside the laboratory.)

4.5 Stratification

There are two different types of stratification to be discussed in the context of engineering: gender stratification and stratification within engineering.

4.5.1 Gender Stratification

Traditional engineering jobs are almost completely job gendered. As computing adopts the name and thus acquires all the connotations of engineering, it is quite possible that job segregation on this scale will start to occur in computing. Computing departments will become departments of engineering and, once most of them have acquired this name, it will be an engineering subject. This word, in spite of the miniature work occurring in electronic engineering for example, still conjures up for women certainly, and maybe for some men as well, images of massive iron foundries, steel works, railway engines, aircraft, military tanks and so on. And when you look at electronic engineering, an engineering subject that does not produce artefacts of this magnitude, at Keele that department had in 1994/5 the same, very low, proportion of women as did computer science.

There is evidence from the US that the percentages of women graduating in computer science courses from within colleges of engineering are, on average, less than the percentages graduating from non-engineering colleges. And if a computer science department moves to a college of engineering then the percentage of degrees awarded to women decreases by between 18 and 26%. (Camp 1997)

My own experience as tutor-in-charge of an MSc course called 'Data Engineering' bears this out. Potential female applicants told me that they were deterred from applying by the word 'Engineering', and a colleague who was working at a recruiting fair in the Far East told me he had the same experience.

4.5.2 Stratification within Engineering

There is stratification within engineering for men. Sally Hacker reports that in her experiences at MIT she found that

> Some fields of engineering – notably electrical and computer science – had more prestige than others. Their activities were clean, hard, and fast. Civil engineering, in contrast was much too messy and encumbered by political and social obstacles for such status. (Hacker 1989, p. 35)

I can see no justification for using the word 'hard' to describe electrical or computing engineering. It would seem to be an attribute men would like to ascribe to computing to bolster its masculine status.

And elsewhere Hacker describes how electronic engineering (EE) carries 'more clout and status than civil engineering'. The former was considered 'cleaner, hardest, most scientific' and the latter far too involved in physical, social, and political affairs. Most engineers agreed with the stereotype of EE, although those outside that field resented its power and status, merely because the field was closer to abstract science.

So those engineers who have status in the traditional fields of engineering are those who work close to abstract science, who are not involved with physical affairs and whose work is clean. To have left the oily rag and dirty hands behind is a sign of status. Now that computing is busy acquiring the status of an engineering subject, similar concerns are arising. I heard someone who calls himself a software engineer suggest that the man who comes to mend the photocopier should not be called an 'engineer'.

Lengthy discussions are taking place within the body of professors and heads of computing in the UK as to how the discipline of computing can acquire the status of engineering and what sort of engineers it will produce.

What are the consequences for women of this stratification in engineering, all the effort required to establish and maintain it and the repetition of all this in computing? The arguments and discussion are almost entirely between men about a male activity. The very fact that discussions occur consolidates the discipline for the participants and establishes a framework into which women have to fit if they wish to enter the new order

4.6 Engineering and the Recruitment of Women

The situation as far as the recruitment of women is concerned should have been eased a little by the fact that as a result of the stratification I have just been talking about we are not trying to recruit into 'oily-rag' engineering. But, on the other hand, the software side of the discipline of computing has adopted the word 'engineering' in order to acquire the masculine identity which traditional engineering already has. Engineering is an aggressive, coercive, interventionist and pervasive activity which is difficult to resist. It is an activity which women have traditionally shied away from.

Computer science has firm roots in mathematics. It is well known that it was the interests of mathematicians like Ada Lovelace and Alan Turing which triggered the development of computers. What is perhaps not so well known yet is how far women were attracted to computing by the mathematical image it projected. Certainly I and a number of my colleagues, both at home and abroad, came into computing via that route. It was the very rules of mathematics which attracted us. Perhaps those male colleagues Maibaum found, those who weren't convinced that computing is an engineering subject, were also attracted to it as a mathematically based discipline. What I am sure of is that if computing moves even further from a mathematics based paradigm towards an engineering paradigm, then even fewer women will engage in it than do at present. And it is no use simply justifying the use of this word 'engineering' by arguing that 'engineering refers to the practice of organising the design and construction of an artefact which transforms the physical world around us to meet some recognised need' – there are other things which matter more than that. The fact that half the population is not present will do for a start.

CHAPTER 5

MATHEMATICS IN COMPUTING: A HELP OR HINDRANCE FOR WOMEN?

This paper was presented in 2000 at the Women, Work and Computerization Conference held in Vancouver (WWC2000)

Abstract

IT HAS ALWAYS BEEN presumed that there are strong links between computing and mathematics and indeed mathematicians did much of the pioneering work for modern computing. But sometimes now these links are given more prominence than their actual role would merit. The fact that both mathematics and computing require abstraction has led to an emphasis on skill in handling abstract ideas which, given the old gendered dichotomy of the practical and the abstract, is of little help to women.

Mathematics is used to bolster the political power of computer 'scientists'. The fact that mathematics underpins sciences like physics, and mathematics underpins computing gives rise to the false impression that computing is a science with all the overtones of masculine dominance that come with a scientific discipline. But computing is not a science. There is an apparent paradox in the fact that the current shift in computing from a mathematical paradigm to an engineering one is deterring even more women than one would expect given that women seem to value the practical aspects of computing.

5.1   The Context

In this chapter I attempt to answer, from a feminist point of view, one of a series of questions about the fundamental nature of computing. Is it a science? Is it an engineering subject? Is it mathematics? Is it all three – or is it none of these? It is the mathematics question that I address here. The allure of science for computing was discussed in Chapter 3 and the influence of engineering was discussed in the previous chapter.

Whatever answers are given to this series of questions, however theoretical and abstract they may appear, they do have a profound influence on men's and women's attitudes to the discipline of computing. I am looking to provide new answers so that we can more effectively challenge the masculinisation of computing. It is not so much whether women like mathematics that I discuss here, it is the role mathematics plays in computing and the influence that that role has on women's attitude to the discipline. Though this paper is not primarily about the attitudes of girls and women as they choose their subjects for higher education, I shall have something to say as a secondary theme about these issues.

5.2   Things Are Not Always What They Seem

It has always been presumed that there is a strong link between computing and mathematics. Indeed it was mathematicians such as Ada Lovelace, Alan Turing and John von Neumann who provided much of the pioneering work leading up to the development of the first modern computers some fifty years ago. The public perception of computers was, until fairly recently, more often than not 'That's about maths isn't it?'. In the schools early personal computers (such as BBC computers in the UK during the first half of the 1980s) were invariably given to the maths departments. And in universities, computing departments often started life within mathematics departments. In some British universities teaching and research in computing is still carried out in departments with names like 'Computing and Mathematics'. The early view of programming languages was that they looked mathematical. Until about ten years ago matriculation level mathematics was considered to be evidence for the type of skills required for studying computing and was therefore an entry requirement for many undergraduate computing courses.

But things are not always quite as they seem. I want for a moment to show how in a parallel case – mathematics in engineering – the links are not purely dictated by intellectual reasoning and this leads to a distorted view of engineering as being highly mathematical. It might look as if mathematics is indissolubly linked to engineering because of the nature of engineering as a discipline. In fact the links are as much political as anything else.

With the establishment of the scientific revolutions of the seventeenth and eighteenth centuries there came an increasing need for young men to demonstrate their rationality and mastery of the mind/body divide. Skill in mathematics came to be seen as proof of this. So mathematics eventually replaced Latin and theology as a general measure of ability. It taught self-discipline and self-restraint. The rules of arithmetic and geometry "will supply accuracy and intelligence for those who follow them" wrote Magistrate La Chalotais in 1793. In 1834 Dr William King, the man appointed as corrector and overseer to Ada Lovelace by her mother, told the 'unruly' Ada that she was to concentrate on mathematics because "her greatest defect is want of order which mathematics will remedy", and because the subject has no connection with feelings and therefore could not possibly raise 'objectionable thoughts' (Woolley 1999, pp. 134–5). So, while Ada Lovelace clearly enjoyed mathematics, the motive for introducing her to it was to discipline her. Mathematics induces "'habits of industry' even if later cast aside, argued a 19th century British cleric" (Hacker 1990, p. 42) .

Mathematics became a 'weeder' or as a professor of mathematics at the University of Toronto put it in 1980

> The main function of mathematics in advanced capitalist society is the maintenance of social stratification. The aridity of our courses, their remoteness from students' human concerns – together, of course, with their difficulty – make them especially forbidding, hence specially good as selectors of students with superior capacity for self discipline (sometimes called repression). (Hacker 1990, p. 139)

Sally Hacker, from whose book many of these quotations are taken, observes how in engineering courses mathematics was taught originally for cultural reasons, not for technical ones.

In the USA in the mid-nineteenth century a struggle developed between a democratic 'shop culture' and an elitist 'school culture'. The shop culture encouraged not only democracy but quality in the development of technical and social skills and 'hands-on' experience. Ability to do mathematics, they argued, was no proof that these young men were good engineers. For them mathematics was not necessary and experience with machines was. On the other hand, for the school culture, also arguing for democracy and quality, skill in mathematics was necessary for a good engineer. The school culture triumphed. And mathematics became a means of distinguishing the 'inferior' shop worker from the engineer. Subsequently the engineering field became overcrowded and in 1926 the engineering profession proposed enrolment limits 'to protect and elevate standards'. The means to limit numbers was mathematical testing.

So there is a long history of including mathematics in curricula for reasons other than its sheer intellectual relevance. On Sally Hacker's view the introduction of mathematics into an engineering education was an instance of this. Perhaps the view that mathematics is an integral part of computing and computing education is yet another instance of giving mathematics a very high profile in a curriculum for reasons other than the sheer intellectual nature of the subject.

My own view is that although there are strong links between mathematics and computing, these have been given more prominence than their actual weight would merit. Plenty of programmers and systems designers are proficient at their jobs without having the mathematical skills needed for complexity theory and discrete mathematics. This exaggeration of the importance of maths is no doubt for 'political' reasons such as, for example, the desire to make computing look more like a science which I shall discuss in more detail later on. What I shall do in the following sections is to distinguish between the actual importance of mathematics and its exaggerated importance and I will offer some ideas as to the reasons for this.

5.3 What Are the Real Links Between Them?

Two factors lead one to expect there might well be a strong link between mathematics and computing. One is the abstract nature of mathematics combined with the fact that certain computing problems can be expressed precisely in an abstract way. The other is the amenability of these computing problems to solution by repetitive processes on machines. However, as we shall see, the links are more complex than that and require some analysis. But I shall first outline two areas where computing is strongly underpinned by mathematics: first, the design and analysis of algorithms and complexity theory and, secondly, discrete mathematics and formal methods. It is important that this underpinning is acknowledged.

5.3.1 Design and Analysis of Algorithms and Complexity Theory

Designing algorithms is about expressing a procedure for, say, sorting an array of numbers in a formal language or a language with a fairly simple but rigorous syntax. Analysis of algorithms is, amongst other things, about finding out how long an algorithm takes to run on a computer. The design and analysis of algorithms is a standard part of computer science curricula.

In 1936 Alan Turing published a paper in which he defined an abstract computer model. This was an abstract machine, which has come to be known as the Turing machine, which Turing then argued could be used to solve all problems. This together with the subsequent development of computers during and after WWII led to the development of a whole new field of mathematics – complexity theory – the identification and classification of problems according to their computational difficulty. This is what Juris Hartmanis (Hartmanis 1995) was referring to when he talked of "quantitative laws that govern the abstract process of computing". These mathematical laws, or rules, can be used to determine how much computer work is needed to execute algorithms. In this context computer work is usually measured by the number of instructions executed and hence the time taken.

There are problems which, according to this mathematical theory, are believed to be *intractable* which means that they will take an impractical amount of computer time to solve, even with conceivable advances in hardware. I say 'believed to be intractable' because nobody has as yet actually proved that this class of problems is not intractable. One example and, a very real one, for parcel delivery or the servicing of networks is the travelling salesperson problem. A travelling salesperson has to visit each city once in a given network and to return to the starting point once all the cities have been visited. The algorithm which has to be devised in this case is one which minimises the distance covered by the salesperson. It takes an unreasonable length of computer time to find the optimum for this, even when the number of cities is quite low.

Another of the many categories of problems identified by researchers in this field of complexity theory are problems which are termed *undecidable*, which means problems for which no algorithm can be written.

5.3.2 Discrete Mathematics and Formal Methods

I mentioned earlier discrete mathematics and the status this has in the curriculum and for the mathematically minded. The major use for discrete maths (which comprises set theory and predicate calculus) in undergraduate courses is in formal methods for software design.

In the late 1960s a 'crisis' was identified in the software industry. This was the result of poor practices in that industry, which resulted in software that didn't work correctly and had to be either abandoned or amended. Some software failures had disastrous consequences. When the crisis was first identified and, new procedures for specifying, designing and writing new software systems were proposed to try to prevent further disasters. The term 'software engineering' was coined because, it was argued, the proposed procedures were parallel to and could be compared with those adopted in the conventional engineering fields e.g. mechanical and civil.

Software development now had to go through phases, typically: requirements analysis, system specification, system design, detailed system design and programming or implementation. The first of these steps, requirements analysis, finding out what the client wants, is probably recorded in text or natural language. But system specification, saying what the system has to do, its functions and the constraints it has to operate under, can be expressed in a mathematical notation. This mathematical notation was embodied in a number of different 'formal specification languages'. Two examples of this type of language are VDM (Vienna Development Method) and Z. Each of these has a different syntax, but the underlying mathematics are broadly the same. The output from system specification is the main input to the system design phase, which defines the architecture of the system.

If, it is argued, the system specification and system design stage are written in a mathematical notation, then they are unambiguous and in principle can be automatically proved (i.e. proven by a computer program) to be correct. The overarching name for this procedure of specifying, designing and verifying or proving correctness is 'formal methods'. Underpinning formal methods is the theory students are taught in discrete mathematics.

On the whole this works so long as systems are completely specified and every eventuality is catered for. For fairly simple closed systems (closed in the sense that they are not at the mercy of, for example, the weather) this method can work. If every eventuality cannot be foreseen and catered for, then the specification is incomplete and it is quite conceivable that it will fail.

W Wayt Gibbs in his aptly entitled article 'Software's Chronic Crisis' suggests another reason for failures of this procedure. He quotes the chairman of one software company as saying [software] engineers rely on mathematical analysis to predict how their designs will behave in the real world. Unfortunately, the mathematics that describes physical systems does not apply within the synthetic binary universe of a computer program; discrete mathematics, a far less mature field, governs here. But using the still limited tools of set theory and predicate calculus, computer scientists have contrived ways to translate specifications and programs into the language of mathematics, where they can be analysed with theoretical tools called 'formal methods'. (Gibbs 1994, p. 77) This suggests that the mathematics used in this branch of computing is immature and its use contrived. And it is not obvious that this branch of mathematics is, at present, by any means always successful, let alone that it can be sufficiently developed to do the job envisaged by proponents of formal methods.

I have provided a, by no means exhaustive, list of the branches of computing in which mathematics is used; for example, the theory underpinning compiler writing is another. However, these topics are not all that computing is about.

5.3.3 But This Isn't All That There is to Computing

There are plenty of topics in computing which don't require mathematics: human-computer interfaces (HCI) is one of them. There is designing of databases using relational database packages which involve school level mathematics. Designing object-oriented databases does not require mathematics. Expert systems don't require mathematics. Systems programming using C, C++ or Java doesn't need mathematics either.

5.4 The Role of Abstraction

One of the criteria often set for admitting people to computer science is whether they can think in the abstract and whether they can express abstract ideas. Matriculation level mathematics, as I have already noted, was once a requirement for entry to most undergraduate computing courses because it was considered to be evidence of skill in abstract thinking and handling mathematical symbolism. The major reason this requirement has been largely dropped is that it only measured skill in some types of abstraction involved in computing but by no means all of them. People who had shown proficiency at matriculation level mathematics were not necessarily good at dealing with the non-mathematical abstractions in computing and, conversely, students could be proficient in the areas of non-mathematical abstraction in computing without necessarily being good at mathematics. In other words, it was not proving as useful a test as people had assumed. In fact only a small part of computer science curricula requires the skill to be able to handle mathematical symbolism. Computing is not only about the topics that require advanced mathematics like complexity theory and analysis of algorithms; as I have just pointed out, it is about other things too, for which skill in mathematics is not a requirement.

In fact everything done on a computer requires some abstraction. If we create a database or a spreadsheet then that is an abstraction of part of the real world; most people are capable of thinking in the abstract to the extent that they can understand these two types of application without knowing much about mathematics and they certainly don't need to understand matriculation maths. That understanding arises out of the fact that non-computing people will learn how to create these abstractions because they have a problem they want to solve. In fact this whole debate about how to get into computing reflects a gender difference of considerable importance in the teaching of the subject. By and large it has been men who favour approaching computing via mathematics and women who favour a more practical approach, even though they like mathematics. Indeed a survey of undergraduate preferences for spending money on a computer as compared with other things showed that young women showed less preference for buying a computer than men of all ages. On the other hand older women showed the same preferences as men. The indications were that perhaps the women had come to value computers for their usefulness (Foreman, Grundy & Lees 1997).

Linda Stepulevage and Sarah Plumeridge interviewed staff giving tutorials for a course on Data Structures. The staff they interviewed, one male and one female, offered two different, and quite common, approaches to teaching this subject. The male tutor described the course as giving students experience in handling data structures so that they can write programs in a systematic methodical way. But real applications are barely mentioned at this level. The female tutor, on the other hand, suggested that the module was too advanced for first year students. 'It's too abstract' she said and they should take it later. She suggested that students should do more programming and become confident in writing code before being introduced to so-called abstract data structures. (I say 'so-called' because the word 'abstract' in this label is redundant – all data structures are abstract. It makes one wonder why the word is there at all.) The male tutor, who also gave all the lectures on data structures, perceived programming as an abstract process akin to mathematics. He, like many other members of the largely male group who control computing syllabuses, wants to keep up the emphasis on abstraction (Stepulevage & Plumeridge 1998).

It is true that abstraction is a useful concept and it is important that we can 'abstract out' of a situation only the details relevant to the task in hand. However, there is a hidden agenda here.

By emphasising abstraction, men can retain control. How can this happen? They suppose themselves to be better at abstract reasoning than women and unfortunately have convinced quite a lot of women that this is so.

One rather extreme example of this is an early twentieth century neurologist, PJ Möbius, who included in a book on talent in mathematicians a chapter on women mathematicians (Möbius 1907). He names some 20 or so female mathematicians and astronomers from Hypatia in the 5th century to Sophia Kovalevskaia and others in the 19th century. Of Hypatia he says, she cannot have produced much of worth because otherwise we would still have it but, he adds, she was a pretty girl and that explains everyone's enthusiasm for her. He gives grudging praise to a few of these mathematicians but this is almost always followed by something that negates the praise; observations such as the way they were helped by relatives or other male mathematicians, or relatives whom they helped in a subordinate capacity. Again and again Möbius says that mathematics is unsuitable for women: they are incapable of reading mathematical texts, they have an aversion to all things numerical, mathematics is the antithesis of femininity, a mathematical woman is contrary to nature, gifted women usually appear dressed like men – Sophia Kovalevskaia (whom we shall meet again in Chapter 9) appeared particularly manly. And so on and on.

The more general tradition of views about the superiority of masculine reasoning, of which this is a rather particular case and something of a caricature, is traced by Genevieve Lloyd in her book *The Man of Reason* (Lloyd 1984). She outlines the views of philosophers such as Plato through Augustine, Bacon, Descartes and others right up to Hegel and Schopenhauer in the 19th century and beyond. She shows how Descartes' Method, for example, required highly disciplined abstract thinking. It was not the case that women were not capable of it, but the prevailing social order made it almost impossible for them to engage in it and anyway their role was to preserve the world of the emotional and the sensuous.

So, there is a very long history of women being regarded as inferior in matters requiring abstraction.

Whenever the requirement for matriculation mathematics was under discussion in my own department a remark I heard so often was 'We want people who are capable of abstract thinking'. Given the well-worn alleged dichotomy of men being good at thinking in the abstract and women being good at the practical, I often felt that the subtext of this statement was 'We only want real men or, at worst, those who can think like real men'.

5.5 The Political Power of Mathematics

We have looked at one political reason for over-estimating the role of maths in computing: the opportunity that it gives men to say that abstraction is crucial to an area and abstraction is what they are conventionally good at.

There are occasions when mathematics is necessary for research but it is also used as a political tool to enhance the reputation of computing research; in other words it is a status symbol. It is arguable whether some research, which is currently labelled research into computing as its proponents would like to think it is, is in fact 'merely' an application of computing. Applied computing is less prestigious than 'pure' computing. The more mathematically oriented a branch of computing is the more theoretical and therefore prestigious it appears. The mathematics and the involvement of pure mathematicians gives such research raised status and a place high in the hierarchy.

Participation in this mathematical computing also gives status to the individuals concerned. Sometimes this status seems to be the only point in including the mathematics. For instance, discrete mathematics is an obligatory part of most undergraduate computer science courses, even though the point of studying these modules is often not evident to those who take them – even when they have finished the course.

Indeed feminist researchers into the teaching of mathematics have noted how the conventional style of teaching at higher levels is one where 'universal truths [are] handed down by some disembodied, non-human force' (Rossi Becker 1995, p. 168) and where lecturers give perfect, error-free lectures from which the student obtains the impression that all mathematics is conducted in this smooth, frictionless way. It is made to seem as though "mathematics provides certain, eternal and universal knowledge arrived at through deductive reasoning and formal proofs" (Schiebinger 1991, p. 170) and (Henrion 1997, Chap. 6). It is mainly male lecturers who teach the mathematics modules in computing and who, in my experience, can use this tradition of expounding unarguable truths to aggrandise themselves as well as making contributions conventionally viewed as valuable to the 'purity' of computing. This 'separated' style of teaching conventional in mathematics as opposed to a 'connected' style has pervaded much of the teaching of computing.

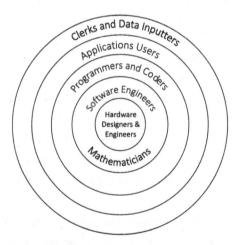

Figure 5.1: *Relationships between mathematics and computing personnel*

Figure 5.1 (a diagram I first developed for the companion paper on computing and science which appears earlier in this volume) shows how computing and its personnel can be viewed as a set of concentric circles. There is a male elite in the innermost circle deciding what the next step in computing shall be and 'discovering', or creating, the truths about computing which they hand out to those who inhabit the outer circles. As you move out from the centre the proportion of women in each circle increases and the power of the members of each circle decreases. For example, in the outermost circle female clerks are featured doing data input; their work practices are completely dictated to them, they have no influence on the product or the processes.

Where does mathematics fit into this scheme? Those interested in algorithms and complexity theory definitely figure in the centre. Other examples like linear programming, Geographic Information Systems (GIS) and CAD fall dangerously near the applied. Those who devise the theory for linear programming, GIS and the graphics for CAD are often pure mathematicians (and I don't mean 'pure' as distinct from applied mathematicians). The computing people who make use of this theory and incorporate it into GIS, CAD systems and so on, use the need for mathematics and the 'purity' of the mathematical theory to give them kudos and near membership of the central elite.

5.6 Does Mathematics Help Make Computing a Science?

In this section I shall argue that computer scientists have used mathematics to make computing look like a science. I shall show how they have done this and why this connection is misleading. This use of mathematics is just one contribution to the notion that computing is a science.

Londa Schiebinger observes that "The prestige of a science often depends on its degree of mathematization, and the more math required for a particular job, the higher the pay and the lower the rate of women's participation" (Schiebinger 1999, p. 171). So, if people can be convinced that computing requires maths in the same way as sciences do, then it is possible that such an apparent requirement will push women out.

Indeed, some people seem to think that because undoubted sciences like physics are underpinned by mathematics and because computing is also underpinned by mathematics in the way I have shown, then computing is a science. But sciences attempt to explain the real world in a rigorous way through setting hypotheses about the real world, collecting data experimentally or through observation and proving or disproving the hypotheses. It is this investigation of the real world that makes, say, physics a science not the use of mathematics, greatly though the use of mathematics may enhance investigations of the real world. As Sandra Harding points out, the price of reducing science to mathematical or logical statements is to contradict perhaps the primary criterion of something being a good scientific claim, namely, that it can be verified or falsified by checking it against the real world. (Harding 1986, p. 52) Peter Denning and his colleagues (Denning et al. 1988) in an ACM report in which they define the discipline of computing, identify two paradigms which form the basis for computer science (which they define as being part of computing). These two paradigms are first, theory, which is 'rooted in mathematics'; secondly, abstraction, which is 'rooted in the experimental scientific method'. This ACM report justifies this use of the word 'abstraction' by saying that, in this respect, computing involves modelling and thus the suppression of non-relevant detail in the way that science does. Indeed, yes, but by itself this scarcely justifies the label 'science'.

What sciences abstract from are objects in the real world. Isaac Newton's identification of laws of motion involved a huge amount of abstraction, for example the inverse square law concerning the acceleration of one body towards another applies to all bodies as diverse as feathers, planets and, even perhaps, apples. The point was, however, that they all have mass however different they are in other, irrelevant respects. But the discovery of Newton's laws of motion was rooted in, and further corroborated by, a great deal of observation of, for instance, planetary motion. Even late in his scientific career when his mathematics was well established, Newton still had to obtain observed data from John Flamsteed, the Astronomer Royal, 'to help prove an aspect of his theory of gravity concerning the orbit of the Moon' (White 1998, p. 313). So that, for all the abstraction involved, these laws were still directly related to objects in the real world, whereas computing's rules (or laws) are about 'endless varieties of computers, algorithms, and languages' which, as Frederick Brooks points out, are tools for others to use in discovering the truth rather than being themselves actual truths about the world (Brooks 1996, p. 62). And it is these actual truths which scientists seek and value for their own sake as distinct from valuing tools as a means to this end.

So, if we leave aside the experimental scientific method and concentrate on the theoretical paradigm, Denning and his colleagues describe what mathematicians do as follows:

1. Characterise objects of study (definition)
2. Hypothesise possible relationships among them (theorem)
3. Determine whether the relationships are true (proof)
4. Interpret results

They continue by saying 'A mathematician expects to iterate these steps, for example, when errors or inconsistencies are discovered.' (Denning et al. 1998, p. 3)

But the objects of study here are not tangible or visible objects from the real world; they have to be defined by people. To imply that we are talking about real things is a sleight of hand which neatly moves mathematics into the world of science. This is achieved by systematic misuse of words like 'hypothesise', 'true' and 'results' and phrases like 'iterate these steps' – mathematicians do not iterate in this way. These phrases are from the world of science and are being used out of their proper context. The association of computing with mathematics is not a way of providing computing with a link to the real world.

Juris Hartmanis (Hartmanis 1995) like all his contemporaries at the forefront of computing through the 1960s and 70s (and as Denning and his colleagues still did at the end of the 1980s as we have just seen) labels the subject he has studied and researched 'computer science'. He describes his search for quantitative laws which govern the behaviour of information and computing but acknowledges that the behaviour of information is not directly governed by physical laws. To talk about 'laws' in this context might seem to be reminiscent of the 'laws of nature' which conventional scientists are seeking but in fact has more in common with the work of logicians. George Boole entitled his celebrated book first published in 1854: *An Investigation into the Laws of Thought, on which are founded the Mathematical Theories of Logic and Probabilities* (Boole 1854); and there are of course de Morgan's Laws and the law of the excluded middle. None of these laws was established by assiduously collecting empirical data. (Alan Turing makes explicit the conventional distinction between 'rules' and 'laws'. He writes "By 'rules of conduct' I mean precepts such as 'Stop if you see red lights', on which one can act, and of which one can be conscious. By 'laws of behaviour' I mean laws of nature as applied to a man's body such as 'if you pinch him he will squeak'" (Turing 1950, p. 452).) So rules are things which you can adopt, but laws are things one has to discover. What I am saying here is that to use the word 'law' is, if one is not careful, to imply that one is discovering laws of nature which operate in the real world as studied by scientists.

However, there is nothing wrong with using the word 'law' so long as one is not misled into thinking that it is a result of empirical study.

What I am saying about mathematics and computing and their relationship to the real world can perhaps be clarified by taking syllogistic logic as a parallel. In syllogistic logic we have an elaborate set of rules about the manipulation of information. For instance, there is a rule which says that it is valid to argue that 'all A's are B's, this is an A therefore it's a B'. There is another rule which says it is not valid to argue that 'all elephants are mammals, mice are mammals, therefore all elephants are mice'. I.e. it is invalid to argue that 'all A's are B's and all C's are B's, therefore all A's are C's'. This elaborate set of rules is, however, not a science. It does not give you any new truth about the world as shown by the fact that it is completely expressible using variables. Indeed logicians insist that they are not concerned with the truth of any premises or conclusions; they are concerned only about the validity of arguments. So it is up to people other than logicians to supply the true premises and then the logicians can tell you how you might validly manipulate this true information. In just the same way computing and mathematics do not themselves supply, or arrive at, truths about the world, but they can tell you how to manipulate information which others, including scientists, provide. Mathematics and computing are no more sciences than logic is and to call computing a 'new science' is to stretch the meaning of the word 'science' very wide indeed. It will not do to broaden the definition of science to include computing as well as the traditional experimental sciences, then as soon as computing is in, to pretend one is still using the word 'science' in its narrow sense. If you let computing in to this list of sciences, then you will have to include logic – and perhaps theology, astrology, alchemy or any systematic study. All this is reminiscent of Edsger Dijkstra's view that computing could be called Very Large Scale Application of Logic. (Dijkstra 1989)

We have seen how mathematics is used in computing. This underpinning by mathematics no more makes computing a science than it makes physics a science. Mathematics helps physicists conceptualise and measure aspects of the real world. But what mathematics does for computing is to help it conceptualise and manipulate a self-referential world of abstractions.

The point of all this is that women are being put off by the labelling of computing as a science when there is no need to give it that label.

5.1   From a Mathematics to an Engineering Paradigm

The early paradigm in computing was a mathematical one, but over the last three or four decades a so-called scientific paradigm crept in and tended to subsume the mathematical one. Now there is a shift to an engineering paradigm. In spite of the fact that science has appeared to dominate computing by, for instance, the use of this label, for many this shift is in fact one from mathematics to engineering.

This change is reflected in a number of ways: the labelling of an increasing number of courses and departments as 'computer engineering', the prominence of software engineering and links between engineers and computer scientists at the professional level, for example giving computing experts official engineering qualifications. Many people fear that there is evidence that this engineering paradigm will deter more women than ever from entering computing. Mathematics will still be there in the computing curriculum but it will be overlaid by an engineering mind-set and all the baggage that comes with that discipline. So, although women can be good at maths and be attracted by the maths that will still be there, the engineering focus of computing will deter a great number of them. (Given Tracy Camp's report from the 1990s showing how the percentage of women graduating in computer science from non-engineering colleges was greater than from engineering based colleges one wonders what effect this movement will have. (Camp 1997))

I have suggested that women value the practical aspects of computing and, for instance, think that this is the way to teach data structures and programming rather than with the emphasis on abstract mathematical approaches. Engineering seems *par excellence* an applied practical activity and yet I, like many others, feel that the engineering paradigm puts women off whereas the abstract mathematics involved in computing is an attraction to many women. This is a paradox.

Traditionally engineering was about realigning matter and forces to fashion large artefacts showing men's power to control parts of nature. The fact that engineering was dirty and dangerous was used to deter women from doing this work, leaving men in control of huge and sometimes deadly artefacts. Women have always been discouraged from traditional engineering by all sorts of means. And this deep-seated belief, that traditional engineering is not a fitting activity for women, is carried over into newer engineering subjects like electronic engineering and computer engineering. It is for this reason – and in spite of the importance that women attach to the practical – that they are deterred from something called 'computer engineering' even if it does only involve software. So that any attraction to computing resulting from the mathematics involved in it is going to be outweighed by the bad image which engineering has for women.

5.8 So Is Mathematics a Help or a Hindrance to Women in Computing?

As we have seen, the answer to this question is not straightforward. There is no doubt that a substantial part of computing is firmly based on mathematics and that some women enter computing because they like maths. But other forces are at work; for example, the emphasis on abstraction to the exclusion of the practical can be a deterrent to women. The apparent 'unarguable truths' of mathematics as it is taught throughout the educational system are replicated in much of the teaching of computing. These factors give mathematics political power and that power extends to the exclusion of women. And then there is the way in which mathematics is used to make computing look like a science, which has the result of firmly embedding computing in a traditionally masculine world.

The answer to the question 'Is mathematics a help or a hindrance to women?' varies over time and with the changing fashions in computing. In the early days some women entered computing mainly because they enjoyed mathematics – I was one of them.

Once mathematics tests become a means of judging computing skills then the attractions for women are likely to decrease as they will too for those women who are fearful of mathematics. And if the advent of the engineering paradigm, with its attendant masculine overtones, increases the volume of mathematical testing in all its pointlessness, then this is likely to deter women even more.

The introduction of alternative syllabuses, with names like 'Informatics', may introduce some pluralism into the ways that computing is presented to those entering higher education. This could enable women to choose approaches which avoid the connotations of engineering or science. But the very real danger then is that men will still choose those options, from the range open to them, which are more 'pure' and masculine, whether they are called 'engineering' or 'science', with their attendant mathematics. The centre will remain intact and largely masculine. Women will still be out on the periphery.

PART III
SOURCES OF POWER

CHAPTER 6

WOMEN, POWER AND PROGRESS

The paper that constitutes this chapter was written while on sabbatical leave at the Technical University of Vienna during the Winter Semester of 2002/3. I would like to express my gratitude both to the Institute for Technology and Society at the T–U Wien for their generous hospitality and to my 'home' department of Computer Science at Keele University in the UK for the time off from teaching that enabled me to write it. And, finally but not least, I must warmly thank the students who attended my seminars and stimulated me to develop these and other ideas.

Abstract

TO REVIEW THE PROGRESS of women in computing is, initially at any rate, depressing. While there is some evidence that there are increasing numbers of women entering some of the traditional sciences at undergraduate level, this increase has not followed through to later career stages. Women are not staying in the scientific professions nor are they being promoted in sufficient numbers. This stagnation prompts an analysis of what really are the goals of women's movements; do they have an ultimate shared goal? Indeed can they have a shared goal at all? One goal, not often articulated,

93

was to give greater recognition and reward to the 'essential' female qualities of nurturing, caring and non-competitiveness. There have been attempts to flatten out hierarchies and to reward these attributes of increased 'connectedness'. The results of such changes are not promising. Not all women have these attributes, many behave in a traditional masculinist way and who is to say these are the 'best' attributes anyway?

Michel Foucault was a proponent of the objections to essential qualities. In order to help understand where power lies and why perhaps change is not taking place at the speed we would all like, I shall examine some of Foucault's ideas. First, there is his proposition that power is everywhere; there is no central point of power. I also relate Foucault's ideas on discipline (the discipline of the body) and normalisation to our lives in the scientific workplace. And I shall provide some contemporary examples of how his description of the technologies of power, discipline and normalisation do indeed appear to operate.

6.1 How Women Are Faring in Science and Technology

Since the early 1990s the central focus of my research had been on the shortage of women in computing and, subsequently, their involvement or lack of it in the design and use of ICTs. In the early 2000s, and after ten years, I was beginning to ask myself what had been achieved in that time. And, to be honest, I had to answer 'not a lot'. To be sure, software and hardware had become sophisticated in a way we would never have dreamed of ten years before and likewise the accessibility of machines. But are women studying computing, are they entering, staying in and moving up the profession? Do they have power and authority within the profession to the same extent as men? The trend in the US, the UK and some Northern European countries, notwithstanding one or two exceptions, is not an upward one. In other parts of the world, for example Eastern

Europe, Mediterranean Europe, India, SE Asia, Africa and Latin America, trends are different. But I shall confine myself to my first list. It can be argued that we could learn lessons from those regions where things are different, but I would like to examine why it hasn't worked 'at home' by which I mean northern Europe. I confine myself to this list because I think this failure raises important questions about essentialism and power that we should be aware of.

Judith Glover in her book *Women and Scientific Employment* (Glover 2000) presents a rather sombre picture from the 1970s (and earlier) through to 1996 from three countries: USA, UK and France. She distinguishes between 'getting in' which means entering the scientific disciplines at school and undergraduate level, 'staying on' which is about not leaving a scientific career after having embarked on one, and 'getting on' or getting promoted. She notes how, since the 1980s, there has been an emphasis on getting women in, or adding more women, to the sciences. There have been such programmes in engineering and computing too. And these programmes have had some successes. But the effect of increasing numbers at these early or 'low' levels ignores the problems of improving male/female ratios further up the hierarchy.

Indeed, even in those sciences where the proportions of women are 50% and over, as for example, the biological sciences, biochemistry and psychology (which she does not mention), the proportions of women higher up the hierarchy are still low. (Incidentally, Glover demonstrates how France is notably different from the USA and the UK.) In other words, in those regions of which I speak there is still vertical gender discrimination in all the sciences and technologies. One lesson from this is that these add-more-women campaigns are only of limited use. Statistics for Higher Education from the UK for the academic year 2000/01 show that just under 10% of professors of science in the UK were female (HESA 2001).

Another disappointment concerns the belief that at one time had currency, namely that once the number of women reaches a critical mass (figures for what is a critical mass vary, some say 15%, others 30% and yet others 50%), then they will start to influence agendas and so on. In the few areas where these sorts of proportions of women have been achieved (biological sciences) there is no evidence that they have had any reforming influence. Accompanying this notion of critical mass is the idea that older women provide role models for younger women thereby giving encouragement. Some of the major proponents of the value of these role models are senior women already in the profession. It is not at all clear on what they base their assertion; in fact the statistical evidence points to the opposite and research into the value of role models points this way as well (Etzkowitz et al. 1994). Research indicated that where there were quite a number of older and senior women, they tended to ally themselves with their male equivalents.

6.2 The Moral Aims of Feminism

There is in fact stagnation creating a malaise within women's movements and this is reflected in and made worse by the lack of agreement on the moral aims of these movements. There is a proliferation of organisations and events whose purpose it seems to me is to add more women, but beyond that there are no well-articulated or shared goals. By 'adding more women' I mean simply that having more women on the payroll, with no accompanying change to the culture or the substance of the discipline, is a quantitative not a qualitative change.

Clearly, feminism can take many forms with different sets of priorities in terms of means and ends. Moreover, as we will see later, it is probably misguided to look for a set of moral objectives, i.e. ends, common to them all. It is not clear that it is possible to have shared goals; maybe it is misguided even to look for them. The absence of any moral aims seems to me to be a crisis to which we are blind except that we can congratulate ourselves on having banished essentialism; this is in theory if not always in practice – I shall say a bit about essentialism in practice in a moment. So, there seems to be a lot of talk about adding more women as if this were the only common ground we could be sure of, possibly realising intuitively the conflicts that would result from trying to actively discuss further moral aims. Donna Haraway talks of "affinity not identity" (Haraway 1985, p. 73) but perhaps antipathy would be as conspicuous as affinity.

6.3 Essentialism: What Does It Mean in this Context?

I shall follow Nancy Goldberger in defining essentialism as the view that there are "enduring, distinctive, and possibly 'natural' or biologically based sex differences" (Goldberger 1998, p. 7).

A classic instance of this essentialism is perhaps Carol Gilligan's comparison of men and women's moral thinking described in her book *In a Different Voice* (Gilligan 1993). She described men as working using the notion of rules, which involved separated, impersonal thinking. Women, on the other hand, she portrayed as being 'connected' and working through compassion rather than impersonal rules.

Kathleen B Jones follows this work of Gilligan's in an analysis of authority. Authority as seen by men ". . . orders existence through rules. Actions and actors are defined by these rules". In the case of women their connectedness results in a compassion which "cuts through the orderly universe with feelings that connect us to [the individuality] of actions and actors. Authority's rules distance us from the person. Compassion pulls us into a face-to-face encounter with another." (Jones 1998, pp. 120–121) In this Kathleen Jones gets at least quite close to attributing essential, and of course differing, qualities to men and to women. Moreover, these are the kind of essential differences that call for changes that break the male monopoly of authority, and that includes changes in our notion of authority. This kind of essentialism suggests a moral programme; a range of changes in ideas, attitudes and practices that ends the lack of opportunity for women to talk in terms of authority.

In this way it looks as if these descriptions of what women really are and what they really think, could form the foundation for a shared morality on which we could base practical changes in society. But even if it were possible to draw up a list of the essential features of women, we would still have the problem of, as the moral philosophers put it, deriving 'ought from is', or deriving moral values and aims from descriptions of how things are. This is easier to see when one is talking about 'human nature' which is often conceived of in less than flattering ways, for instance human beings are often seen as inherently selfish. Clearly one would not just want to read off a set of moral values from such a description of human beings. Some facts are welcome and some are regrettable and the classification of them as good or bad is more than can be established from the facts by themselves.

Not only is getting 'ought' from 'is' problematic, but so too is getting the 'is' in the first place. We cannot say that all women possess such and such an attribute. As Donna Haraway says "There is nothing about being 'female' that naturally binds women" (Haraway 1985, p. 72). Women are social constructs; as Simone de Beauvoir famously wrote: "One is not born a woman, but, rather, becomes one" (de Beauvoir 1988, p. 295). What 'essentialists' were often doing was not reading off a set of values from 'the facts', but rather reading into their description of the facts the values that they wanted to see there; typically, qualities like nurturing, caring and non-competitiveness. Even if one had a list of essential female qualities, there would still be the moral question of which items in this list could be classified as 'good'.

6.4 Michel Foucault

In this chapter I shall examine some of the ideas of the French philosopher Michel Foucault because he also had come to the conclusion that there is no essential nature of people. He also concluded that it is impossible to derive a universal morality from facts. Religion and law had, in his view, lost their plausibility as grounds of ethics.

Indeed he argued that "The search for a form of morality acceptable to everybody in the sense that everyone should submit to it strikes me as catastrophic." (Diamond & Quinby 1988, p. xiii). And yet Foucault was not dismayed by this and, as we shall see, proposes an ongoing struggle. Although Foucault had little to say about the position of women, his ideas are applicable to their relative position *vis-à-vis* men and have provided a rallying point for feminists. Let us examine why.

As Irene Diamond and Lee Quinby point out in the introduction to a collection of papers they have edited entitled *Feminism and Foucault*, one striking area of agreement between feminism and Foucault is that "both identified the body as the site of power, that is, as the locus of domination through which docility is accomplished and subjectivity constituted" (Diamond & Quinby 1988, p. x); hence the importance of sexuality to both Foucault and feminists. The starting point for his three-volume work on the history of sexuality was the all pervasiveness of sexuality in modern society.

Sexuality, Foucault argues, is a historical social construction, or an apparatus "designed to mould sexual practices towards certain strategic and political ends" (McHoul 1977, p. 77). These ends are to promote the goals of the bourgeoisie. They are achieved partly through taking over the physical bodies of individuals and also controlling the population as a whole. For example, the Victorian ideal of marriage encouraged sex and procreation in the privacy of the home, which meant control in terms of who had sex with whom and the time spent in such activities. There were all sorts of other advantages for the bourgeoisie in a capitalist society. To summarise this I quote Foucault himself: "The disciplines of the body and the regulations of the population constituted the two poles around which the organisation of power over life was deployed." (Foucault 1988, p. 139) The two together he termed 'bio-power'.

Women and men's fashions, body language and other aspects of behaviour confirm their sexuality. Foucault's ideas have been applied by feminists to issues like the normalising role of female fashions (for example, tight fitting bodices, foot binding, high heeled shoes), body language (while women take up little space, men are expansive), male and female cosmetics, and cosmetic surgery. (See, for example (Bratky 1988).) Foucault's ideas have also been used to gain insight into the complex backgrounds of gender and eating disorders (e.g. anorexia, bulimia) and of gender and rape.

In all issues of the type that interest feminists and that Foucault actually commented on, his view was that the body is of paramount importance. He argued forcibly that the body is not something given and biologically fixed, but has been modified in various ways and over long periods of time. What happens is that, by a process of normalisation, men and women are convinced that the current defining criteria of how the body should be actually describes the biologically normal and therefore ideal body, thus presenting a norm for people to aspire to. Society uses various pressures to encourage each of us to adopt this norm as standard. Those who fail are judged and often informally punished for failing to reach them. These notions of the pressures exerted and the punishments meted out form an important theme in what I shall be saying.

These are the kinds of things that made feminists look to see what Foucault says about common aims, if there are any, for women. To follow this through we must talk briefly about the notion of power since that was crucial in Foucault's thinking.

6.5 Power

6.5.1 Sources and Directions of Power

Foucault's unravelling, or deconstruction, of power clarifies how power operates. He deconstructs the traditional view of power, which was that it is a purely negative force, something that is synonymous with repression, and promotes it as a positive force. So, in Foucault's view power is much more than merely repressive. Another important feature in his view of power is that it is not unidirectional; it is everywhere. "Power is everywhere; not because it embraces everything, but because it comes from everywhere." (Foucault 1988, p. 93) In an interview he said

> When I think of the mechanics of power I think of its capillary form of existence, of the extent to which power seeps into the very grain of individuals, reaches right into their bodies, permeates their gestures, their posture, what they say, how they learn to live and work with other people. (Sheridan 1980, p. 217)

Power, as he perceives it in the modern world, is not simply exerted from above. "Power comes from below . . ." (Foucault 1998, p. 94) Neither the state, nor the law, nor other institutions are the origins of power but they are "an overall strategy and effect" (Martin 1998, p. 6). It's no use looking for a centre of power or a central power. The UK laws concerning discrimination on the grounds of gender and race provide a good example of the way a central power is in fact powerless. Laws against gender and race discrimination and one that is supposed to enforce equal pay have been in force in the United Kingdom for some 50 years. (The Sex Discrimination Act 1975 (UK), the Race Relations Act 1965 (UK) and the Equal Pay Act 1970 (UK) have subsequently been repealed and their provisions incorporated into other legislation.)

6.5.2 Discipline and its Normalising Effects

In medieval society power was exercised by, and in the name of, a sovereign who had ultimately the power of death over his or her subjects. According to Foucault, this somewhat 'external' model of control has been replaced by another model whose main function is to control lives more thoroughly. In this modern scheme this control is exercised through the discipline of the body. Disciplining the body is of course one of the poles of Foucault's bio-power that I mentioned earlier. In schools, prisons, the military, hospitals, police forces, administrations and in units of employment, people are observed, measured, compared and thereby disciplined. (Sheridan 1980, pp.192 -193) (Modern day 'call centres' are a striking example of this.) One result of continued observation, be it of the prisoner, patient or employee, is that eventually they discipline themselves. In other words the discipline comes from within. As Foucault wrote ". . . the perfection of power should tend to render its actual exercise unnecessary" (Foucault 1977, p. 201). And part of this process of observation and measurement is the collection of knowledge about individuals. This gives rise to notions of power/knowledge: knowledge about individuals gives other people power over them. Power/knowledge is another topic that Foucault discusses and one that I am not going into at length now except to make a brief point.

This collection of knowledge through measurement and so on is the basis for setting norms and for recognising the dividing line between the 'normal' and the 'abnormal' – this is an important function in an organisation whose aim is 'the administration of life'. These observations and data supply the basis for categorising people and their varying degrees of 'deviance'. So, once the rules are set, they can be used to judge people.

Rather than a division between loyal subjects on the one hand and enemies of the sovereign on the other, we now have a division between the normal and the abnormal. In fact the division isn't quite as binary as that; we now have a norm that eventually produces a calibrated, measured, hierarchical society. A society that normalises its subjects is the historical effect of a technology of power centred on the body, hence the importance of sex as a political issue.

> This bio-power was without question an indispensable element in the development of capitalism; the latter would not have been possible without the controlled insertion of bodies into the machinery of production and the adjustment of the phenomena of population to economic processes. (Foucault 1998, pp. 140–141)

Instead of the more external influence of the sovereign and his laws we now have a whole set of internalised norms, which police our behaviour, appearance, our whole lives in fact. And the more our lives are regulated by society and "The judges of normality are present everywhere . . . the teacher-judge, the doctor-judge, the educator judge, the 'social-worker' judge" (Foucault 1977, p. 304) to which he could have added employer-judge, the more knowledge is gained by these processes. The exercise of power and the accumulation of knowledge are two sides of one process.

Just as Foucault argues that power is not only repressive, he also holds these processes of normalisation do not produce conformity. "We must not make the mistake of thinking that techniques of power have crushed those natural forces which mark us as distinct types of human beings with various 'personality' traits. Rather, differences, peculiarities, deviances and eccentricities are ever more highlighted in a system of controls concerned to seek them out." (McHoul 1977, p. 72) On the face of it this appears somewhat paradoxical. On the one hand he is saying people are being made to conform to some norm and, on the other hand, he is saying that this very process highlights differences. What I think is happening here is that differences are highlighted in order to make people conform. (See (Foucault 1977, pp. 182–183).)

Now I give a few examples of how we are controlled through the power of the norm. Anne Fausto-Sterling's book *Sexing the Body* provides a compendium of detail on the efforts of the medical profession to use the notion of a norm to enable them to get intersexuals to fit into "one or the other cubbyhole" (Fausto-Sterling 2000, p. 8). She has a telling cartoon to illustrate this (p. 59).

People who want sex changes have to show the medics that they really want to become a 'real' woman or man by cross-dressing before they are allowed to have surgery. For a man-to-woman change the pressure is on the client to behave according to some notion of a 'woman' if they want the surgery. Who supplies this notion of a 'real' woman?

I have already mentioned the controlling effects of fashions on men and women. Many of us, and I am as guilty as anyone, conform to these fashions to a large extent. Having said that many people conform, we do each have our little pockets of resistance that change over time.

Sophisticated women still discuss how to dress for job interviews. Should they wear a short skirt, how much make-up should they wear, do they have to wear a bra? My initial reaction to this discussion was why on earth is it still happening? We are still sexualised and this discussion is part of the continuing sexualisation process. But as far as normalisation is concerned it does represent a point at which what is normal is being debated. Was one objective of the discussion to establish a norm for dress code? Whether it was or not the discussion was still against the backdrop of women's sexuality and the way in which the interviewees were to make it visible or invisible to the interviewers

6.5.3 Resistance to Power

Just as power comes from a multiplicity of centres, so too does resistance to that power. Just as there is no centre of power, so no frontal attack on the state is going to work and a quite different form of struggle has to be adopted. The struggles must be "local [ones] that undermine institutional power . . . as it operates in homes, schools, prisons, therapists' offices and factories, wherever the work of normalization is carried on." (Martin 1988, pp.9–10)

Indeed, Foucault refuses to suggest grand solutions and only refers to these local struggles, and when asked if he would propose something, replied

> My position is that it is not up to us to propose. As soon as one 'proposes' – one proposes a vocabulary, an ideology, which can only have the effects of domination. What we have to present

are instruments and tools that people might find useful. By forming groups to make these analyses, to wage these struggles, by using these instruments or others: this is how, in the end, possibilities open up.

But if the intellectual starts playing once again the role that he has played for a hundred and fifty years – that of prophet, in relation to what 'must be', to what 'must take place' – these effects of domination will return and we shall have other ideologies, functioning in the same way (Foucault & Kritzman 1988, p. 197)

Far from working to fulfil some universal moral aim, Foucault in the last phase of his thinking suggested an aesthetic mode of life in which each should "search for styles of existence as different from each other as possible" (Diamond & Quinby 1988, p. xii). So, this gives some clue as to how to choose what actions to take and which power-points to resist and what form this reaction should take. We should make choices on the grounds of aesthetics. Instead of the universal moral rules he rejects, he calls for diversity in life-style.

6.5.4 Foucault's Optimism

There are large elements of cheerfulness in Foucault in spite of aspects that initially might look pessimistic. There is, for instance, little sense of progress in his writing. Certainly, he is poles away from any sense of a golden age just around the corner in the way Marxism postulated. He would reject strongly the view that history is going inexorably towards a great culmination and one that was global in its scope. Nevertheless there is still the opportunity to engage in local struggles with limited aims and "It is simply in the struggle itself and through it that positive conditions emerge." (Foucault & Kritzman 1988, p. 197)

We have already seen an example of his cheerfulness or

optimism in his rejection of the idea that the process of normalisation produces only conformity. Another example of his cheerfulness is that, although it might look as if power is repressive, Foucault chides those who put too much emphasis on that aspect. He wrote

> We must cease once and for all to describe the effects of power in negative terms: it 'excludes', it 'represses', it 'censors', it 'abstracts', it 'masks', it 'conceals'. In fact, power produces; it produces reality; it produces domains of objects and rituals of truth. (Foucault 1977, p. 194)

6.6 One That Got Away

6.6.1 Some More Foucault and a Story

I would like to tell a story concerning the way in which feminist work has been received in one traditional scientific department. I want to tell this story because so much of it reflects some of Foucault's ideas on power and so on.

First, I need to amplify what he said about the role of sexuality in our society. Sexuality has become an instrument of power. "It appears rather as an especially dense transfer point for relations of power: between men and women, young people and old people, parents and offspring, teachers and students, priests and laity, an administration and a population" (Foucault 1998, p. 103). Let's pause for a moment on the phrase 'dense transfer point'. Every interaction between say two people takes place against a background of an awareness (conscious or unconscious) of their gender and sexuality. And if one is older than the other, then that age difference is another feature of this sexuality. Similarly with parents one will be conscious of their gender when interacting with them. Thus the phrase 'dense transfer point' refers to the volume of traffic that is always present in these relationships of power.

The mechanisms by which sexuality has attained its centrality since the beginning of the eighteenth century are fourfold. They include the hysterisation of the female, which, according to Foucault, involved the medicalisation of their bodies. (Foucault 1998, p. 104) "For centuries [women] were told: 'You are nothing but your sex. And this sex, doctors added, is fragile, almost always sick and always inducing illness.'" (Foucault & Kritzman 1988, p. 115) So, I interpret 'medicalisation of their bodies' to mean that the female body became a legitimate focus of attention on the part of the medical profession, including the newly emerging psychiatric profession. Interestingly the word 'hysteria' was introduced in English in 1801 as meaning:

> A functional disturbance of the nervous system . . .
> and usually attended with emotional disturbances
> of the moral and intellectual faculties. Women
> being more liable than men to this disorder, it was
> originally thought to be due to a disturbance of the
> uterus. (Shorter Oxford English Dictionary)

"[T]he Mother, with her negative image of 'nervous woman', constituted the most visible form of this hysterization." (Foucault 1998, p. 104). This 'idle' woman "inhabited the outer edge of the 'world', in which she always had to appear as a value, and of the family, where she was assigned a new destiny charged with conjugal and parental obligations" (Foucault 1998, p. 121). So, as well as the medicalisation of women's bodies, there is also focus on their role within the family.

As I have explained, Foucault argues that since the beginning of the 18th century, there has arisen a new discipline of the body in schools, the military, prisons. In modern times he argues people are coerced into disciplining themselves. The hysterisation of women would presumably be part of this move to get people to discipline themselves in order to avoid opprobrium from society. This goes along with discipline in schools, the military, places of employment and so on. Another observation of Foucault that is relevant for the story I am about to tell is that of the interaction between the law and the medical profession. Foucault's book entitled *I, Pierre Rivière, having slaughtered my mother, my sister and my brother ... A Case of Parricide in the 19th Century* provides all the available documentary evidence relating to the murder of three members of his family by a 20-year-old man, Pierre Rivière, in 1835. (Foucault 1978) The documentary evidence includes that of doctors and lawyers. To summarise with some simplicity their views, the doctors found him insane and the judicial system that he was of sound mind. This evidence and the ensuing notes by Foucault and some colleagues set the murders, the trial and other events against the complex background of the French Revolution, the then emerging field of psychiatry and the current political atmosphere (including other contemporaneous trials for murder). The point of my mentioning this is not that it has directly to do with gender, but with the conflict and tensions that were beginning to emerge at the start of the 19th century between the medical and legal domains in determining what madness is.

Now to my story, which is about my own experiences. As I recount some of them, I shall try to relate these events to Foucault's theories. There has been a constant tendency over the last thirty or so years within my working environment to cast my views, my research, and my life style as abnormal. In other words, the scene was set long ago.

The Sex Discrimination Act became law in the UK 1975 (this Act was subsequently replaced by other legislation) and four years later in 1979 I won a legal case against my employer, a university, for their failure to promote me on the grounds of my sex. Employment cases like this are heard before special tribunals. These operate without the ceremony of the higher courts and the idea, when they were set up in the 1970s, was that individual employees could bring their complaints and appear before them in person. They were supposed to be accessible to the individual and to operate without lawyers. However, very quickly the employers started to use lawyers to defend themselves.

I engaged a lawyer, as did my employer. After I won, the reaction to my winning from senior people within the university was denial. First, they tried to deny that it was a legal win, for example, one senior person enclosed the word 'legal' in quotation marks when writing about it, thus trying to undermine its legality. Some said that I had lost, and many said I had brought the university into disrepute – remember, I had won and it was the university which was found wanting. I received the minimum redress in that I was promoted; there was no financial compensation. After that, they just waited for a short period and things went back to normal. In some respects the ramifications of this are still very much present, partly because of the myths that grew out of the outcome, so the benefit I derived from using the law was minimal. In Foucauldian terms there are two points to make here. The first is that I tried to exercise power by taking the case and by winning it. Then my employer resisted this win and in turn exercised power by denial. The second point that I derive from Foucault is that the law is not a straightforward source of power. A win in law brought me little benefit.

In order to complete setting the scene I should add that I have also been an active trade unionist since 1979. I do all sorts of different work in this respect for men and women and am involved in a case involving a male lecturer accused of sexual harassment.

There is also a UK law[9] that is designed to protect people who engage in trade union activities. Again, as you will see, this is ineffective.

Next came my research into gender that I started in 1991/92. I work in a very traditional Computer Science department. It was interesting that while all around me people were doing research into gender in French literature, English literature, Russian literature, in history, philosophy and law nobody could accept that there was a problem in the sciences – least of all computing. The more publicity

I got the more there were mutterings about getting me to stop this work – 'we must be careful', 'we must stop her doing this' and so on. There was also the inevitable ridicule. My colleagues read very little of what I write, let alone discuss it in any depth.

I applied for promotion. It was bizarre. They ignored my referees, got their own and then ignored what the positive ones wrote. My application failed and I appealed. That process took the better part of two years and it failed. What I did hear was that it had been decided at a senior level that I would not be promoted because of my continuing trade union activities. I have no proof of this; I understand that a lot of evidence was destroyed, but it is reasonable to infer that this was a reason for their failure to promote. Most people who get involved in trade union work give it up at some point and then get promoted. I didn't, so I wasn't 'normalised'. Again, the law did not seem to act as a deterrent.

I still didn't give up my trade union work and I didn't apply again for promotion. My employer's next moves are really interesting if we look at them in the context of Foucault. I was deemed to be ill. I have seen an assertion that I was sick and needed to 'see a doctor'. They kept asking me to go and see a doctor of their choice which I refused to do. One email I saw said that the author had suggested that what I really needed was medical help and, since I vehemently refused these 'offers of help', the time had come to start disciplinary proceedings against me. And it was never said what I had done to require disciplining. Here there was confusion as to whether I was 'mad or bad'. I was clearly way outside some expected norm. At one meeting with a senior member of staff there was also a strong implication that I should retire and look after my husband and my elderly father. I.e. one way I could 'save my soul' and return to normality was to take my proper place in my family.

There was a further side-show. They started a risk assessment. Usually risk assessments are for employees who may themselves be at risk from using chemicals, radioactive materials or are required to do heavy lifting or have to enter confined spaces and so on. This so-called risk assessment was interesting because the idea of risk became inverted and it was to ascertain whether or not I was a health risk to others. I saw a report in which my head of department suggested that he was concerned for the safety of the department and indeed for his own safety. Under pressure I agreed to see the occupational health physician who declared me normal. As a result my employer stopped trying to get me declared 'sick'. However, they ignored the physician's advice to have an open discussion. But it's interesting that that theme could ever have been seriously entertained; that I was a threat, a danger to public health. Psychiatry was being used in Foucault's phrase as a "sort of public hygiene" (Foucault & Kritzman 1988, p. 134).

These are few of the things that happened to me, there were others too, but these are more tangential in their relevance to Foucault.

6.6.2 What Should We Do?

As far as the absence of a universal morality is concerned, Foucault suggests criteria of aesthetics, matters of taste rather than morality. He suggests that the question is not 'am I living a morally good life?' but 'am I leading an aesthetically pleasing life or is it in good taste?' He talks about his own intensity of pleasure; the decisions to be made are matters of taste and not of morality i.e. we do not expect to dispute about them. Nevertheless one can feel very strongly about them, for example, for things one doesn't like: 'I cannot stomach them', 'they're disgusting' or more colloquially 'they make me feel sick' or less strongly 'they're distasteful'.

Like Foucault, I don't believe the answers are moral ones. For my own part, I sometimes think I'm looking for justice for women, but in reality I'm looking first and foremost for something that pleases me. We have, as individuals, to look at our own lives and define what is aesthetically pleasing for us and strive towards that.

To conclude, Biddy Martin points out that the women's movement has been criticised for fragmentation, lack of organisation, absence of a coherent theory and the inability to mount a frontal attack. Foucault has argued persuasively that these were not realistic goals and that there is much more potential in the kind of view he has of things than there is in the centralisation and abstraction that critics like those whom Biddy Martin quotes still seem to be looking for. (Martin 1988, p. 10)

CHAPTER 7

UNIVERSITY PROSPECTUSES: IS THERE A HIDDEN MESSAGE FOR WOMEN?

Reprinted from Journal of Women and Minorities in Science and Engineering, Volume 6, Issue 4, 2000, Frances Grundy, University Prospectuses for Computing: Is there a Hidden Message for Women? pages: 331–348, with kind permission from Begell House, Inc. DOI: 10.1615/JWomenMinorScienEng.v6.i4.40

Abstract

CRITICAL DISCOURSE ANALYSIS IS a technique for analysing power relations within texts and against the backgrounds of other texts, spoken and written. Given the low proportions of women entering computing in many countries, this study uses this technique to analyse one of the first formative points of contact between prospective female students of computing, on the one hand, and computing departments on the other – namely, university prospectuses. The backdrop to this is the common view of computing as a scientific/ engineering/mathematical subject, which also requires the use of technology. All these are traditionally male-dominated fields of expertise. The analysis of two departmental prospectuses uncovers the interweaving of these preconceptions with the text which is distributed to prospective students; this includes the influence of 'prestigious' scientific research. These and other aspects seem to be likely deterrents to many women. Some suggestions are offered as to how our understanding of the situation might be improved. For example, we particularly need more work on the influence of the science/engineering paradigm in computing on women.

7.1 Introduction: Critical Discourse Analysis

"All representations of events are *polysemic* – that is ambiguous and unstable in meaning – as well as a mixture of 'truth' and 'fiction'. Despite the desire of some writers to be utterly truthful and accurate, we are unwittingly trapped in a world of biased perceptions and 'stories', all of which both exceed and shortchange 'reality'." (Riggins 1997, p. 2)

One of the roles of discourse analysis is to reveal the 'fiction' to those for whom it is wholly or partly hidden. It is the systematic study of the interaction of various types of discourse, discourse events, or, more simply, texts. These may be pieces of text from books, newspaper articles, speeches, recorded conversations, e-mail messages, pages on the World Wide Web (WWW), academic lectures, instructions on how to operate a piece of software, and, for this article, university prospectuses.

Discourse analysis is the analysis of the different components of text – lexicogrammatical, semantic, pragmatic. At the same time, it takes into account the social contexts in which these texts are produced; that is to say, discourse analysis is the study of 'intertextuality'. "All statements are intertextual because they are interpreted against a backdrop of other statements" (Riggins 1997, p. 2).

Within certain domains, analysts can find a certain consistency in the expression of ideas that reflect the current understanding of that domain. Intertextual analysis strengthens the picture of the domain. It links the text to the context in which the former has been created.

Power and dominance, as evidenced in racism and sexism, are reflected in and reinforced by discourse. Critical discourse analysis (henceforth CDA) "is an instrument whose purpose is to expose power structures" (Wodak 1997, p. 7). Or, again, as Norman Fairclough and Ruth Wodak put it:

> So discourse may, for example, be racist, or sexist, and try to pass off assumptions (often falsifying ones) about any aspect of social life as mere common sense. Both the ideological loading of particular ways of using language and the relations of power that underlie them are often unclear to people. CDA aims to make more visible these opaque aspects of discourse. (Fairclough & Wodak 1997, p. 258)

They continue by saying that CDA is not dispassionate, objective social science but is a form of intervention in social practice by people who are committed opponents of racism or sexism, for example. CDA exposes the usually hidden mechanisms whereby attitudes are created and reinforced by, for instance, the choice of vocabulary (nouns, verbs, adjectives, and pronouns), the order in which ideas are presented, the choice of voice (active or passive), the choice of accompanying illustrations – indeed all those ways of manipulating people into accepting the present power structure as 'only natural' (West, Lazar & Kramarae 1997, p. 127).

A few examples of CDA that uncover power relations may be helpful at this point. Candace West in West et al. (p. 124) quote Kate Clark's study (Clark 1992) of reports of rape in the *Sun* (a British tabloid). These texts obscure the guilt of the rapist by, for example, using passive sentence structures that delete the rapist as agent: "Two of Steed's rape victims — aged 20 and 19 — had a screwdriver held at their throats as they were forced to submit." Also, by using

115

passive sentences they transfer the blame to somebody else: "Sex killer John Steed was set on the path to evil by seeing his mother raped when he was a little boy." These texts also describe the victims of rape in a way that might be excusing the rapist, for example, as an "unmarried mum" or a "blonde divorcee".

It is important to reiterate that those engaging in CDA take an explicit political stance. They take the standpoint of those who hitherto have not identified the hidden messages in these texts and who are disadvantaged by their presence. This is true of the analysis of university prospectuses that follows.

7.2 The Backdrop

The low proportion of women studying computing is well documented. The percentage of women students studying for computing degrees is 10% in a sample of Australian universities (personal communication from Paula Roberts, 5 August 1999), 9.5% in 1993–1994 (Oechtering & Behnke 1995) and 8.7% in 1995 (Schinzel 1997) in Germany, below 10% in Norway (Rasmussen 1997), 10% in Sweden for the first half of the 1990s, and rising to 18% for beginners in 1996 (Bjorkman et al. 1997) and 10.9% in the United Kingdom in 1993–1994 (Grundy 1996). These are all less than 20% of the computing student population and, in some individual institutions, the figure is even lower. In the United States, the figure in 1993–1994 was 28.4% (Camp 1997). In the present study, I have examined an example of discourse from one country England (although only a part of the UK), as we have just seen, these proportions are low.

A number of hypotheses have been put forward to explain the small proportion of women students of computing: (a) computer games designed almost entirely for boys, which they start playing at a very early age; (b) differing attitudes of teachers to boys and girls in technical subjects; (c) differing attitudes of parents to sons and daughters; boys and men (not necessarily their fathers) using technology, such as computer hardware, for 'bonding' purposes; (e) computer jargon and its undertones of violence and sexual aggression; (f) computer magazines for which the male readership is in the region of 80 to 90% (Grundy 1996, p. 19).

A further factor that might contribute to an explanation of the poor figures is the practice of describing and perceiving computing as a science-, engineering-, and/or mathematics-based discipline. These three subjects have different connotations for men and for women. For example, there are very few women engineers, and these gender-based connotations must therefore influence women's views of computing. When looking at these subjects in a very general way, women may have different views of science and engineering, on the one hand, and mathematics on the other. These three subjects cannot be treated in the same way. In this study, I am concerned with the influence of science and engineering and not with that of mathematics. I am not suggesting that all women are deterred by these connotations, but rather that many prospective female students are. Nor am I suggesting that these are the only factors – there are others at work, too, and I shall discuss some of them.

As I have already noted, the traditional Baconian idea of Western science in which man the scientist probes Nature, which is so often personified as female, has laid the ground for women being deterred from scientific study. Other traditions in the natural sciences, such as the subject/object split, objectivity, and the study of objects 'out there' – the requirement that emotions must not be allowed to influence the scientific process – are further factors which deter women from entering science. But computing is not a science in this traditional sense, and to appropriate that title is not only questionable for intellectual reasons but has the crucial consequence of deterring women in much the same way as the traditional sciences have done.

The enthusiasm for calling computing a science is on the wane to a certain extent (although its influence is still strong), and the tendency nowadays is to label it an engineering subject. This I shall illustrate shortly. There is more justification for the appropriation of this word than for that of 'science'. But it is still an appropriation of something with intensely masculine overtones. Traditional engineering – military, civil, and mechanical – is about realigning forces and matter often to make large, domineering, and sometimes deadly artefacts. Until very recently, women never became involved in engineering without great sacrifice. To appropriate this word is to carry over all the symbolism of 'engineering' and some of its other influences, too: professional associations or brotherhoods and the attendant scatological and sexual humour that denigrates the body and minorities.

In all university prospectuses, computing (in the 'pure' sense that I wish to discuss it here) is classified either as a science or an engineering subject or both. For example, most of the degrees offered in computing are Bachelors or Masters of Science or Engineering. But I shall also be looking at the emphasis that the prospectuses put on these two disciplines as they introduce the subject to prospective students.

It is against this background that I examine the prospectuses; it is the intertextuality of perceptions of science and engineering and the connotations that these have for women that I investigate in these prospectuses.

7.3 University Prospectuses as Text

There are many modes of discourse within academic computing that can be used for a study of power relations. One can examine spoken communication, for example, computer talk between staff and students outside formal teaching situations. One can look at text books, journals, staff web pages – in short, all documentation used for addressing students. My present primary concern is why so few women take up computing in England when they enter higher education. One of their earliest points of contact is the undergraduate prospectus, and it is a study of these that I am presenting here. How off-putting are they to women as compared with men? What hidden messages are there in these apparently straightforward and gender-innocent texts? How might they be written to encourage women's entrance to the profession?

All university prospectuses have some common features. As well as being available as glossy printed booklets, many are now also on the WWW. The material in both is normally the same; in fact, the same text and pictures are often used for both media. Although prospective students do use the Internet as well as advice from teachers and parents, the printed prospectuses are seen as one of the most important influences (*Guardian Higher*, Tuesday 23 March 1999, p. iv).

In these prospectuses, the division of the texts is almost identical: the institution and its location, the faculties, the departments, courses offered, and the qualifications to be attained (Bachelor of Science, Bachelor of Arts, etc.), the syllabuses for these courses, the career opportunities for graduates of each course, and facilities for social activities, sports, shopping, and so on. Many include the experiences of alumni or, alternatively, pieces by students still at the institution giving their views on how they find it.

The primary aim of all these prospectuses is to attract as many applicants as possible – to 'sell' the programs. Education is commodified in and by these documents. There are conventions for the presentation of all this information, not just to make it easier for the student to locate the information they need, but also because there are standards to be maintained among institutions within national boundaries. Conventions and similarities are also present in entries for computing. Most departments have words like 'science' and 'engineering' in their titles, students will become Bachelors or Masters (both masculine titles, see (Grundy 1996, p. 92, footnote 7)) of Science or Engineering, and they will work in 'laboratories'. These conventions should be analysed. But I shall also look for subtleties in the text that 'speak' to men and that may be read in a different way by women. The photographs and illustrations in these prospectuses also serve a purpose. Some, particularly those of the area surrounding the institution and those representing social activities, remind one of an advertisement for tourist attractions. But there are other messages in these pictures, and these should be analysed also.

7.4 The Prospectuses Chosen

I sought printed prospectuses from 10 English universities, all of which offered computing: five 'new' and five 'old' universities. It would be a help in understanding what follows if I now sketch fairly recent changes and some of the political forces affecting funding for British universities. The universities that are still often categorised as 'new' are largely former polytechnics that acquired university status around 1992.

Traditionally, these institutions were teaching-oriented, vocational institutions, which placed less emphasis on research than the 'old' universities (those which already had university status in 1992). As I shall observe later, excellence in research is generally more highly valued than excellence in teaching, and research attracts funding and hence better and more up-to-date equipment. Funding is obtained, not only from sources external to the higher education system but also from central sources, as a direct result of excellence in research; there is a regular research assessment exercise (RAE) in which departments are judged by panels of peers.[10] Those universities with high RAE ratings attract more kudos as well as greater funds than those with low ratings.

From the point of view of discourse analysis, the prospectuses from the new universities seem to be conveying identical messages. They almost all list the syllabus content of degree programs. They are written in a concise, informative style of text, which is almost uniform between prospectuses. The photographs are lively, showing students engaged in work, and there is a good mix of different races and gender. These institutions look like happy places where students enjoy life and work hard. Because the uniformity and the brevity of their course descriptions are not rich seams for analysis, none of them were used.

The old universities have a wider range of textual styles – one as short and succinct as some of those from the new universities and some without detailed lists of syllabus content in the main prospectus. One was particularly eye-catching and richly produced with colour photographs. Three came with extra departmental brochures where syllabus content was given if it did not appear in the main prospectus. For the purposes of critical discourse analysis I chose, from this range of presentational styles, two that are from different ends of the spectrum of the degree of effort they made to make their courses attractive to women. Other analysts might have made a different decision about what 'spectrum' implies, but that does not undermine what I have to say about these two prospectuses in particular.

The first of the universities I shall call University A Founded in 1907, this one is located in central London and is part of London University but, like other London colleges, is generally considered to be a university in its own right. Its name implies that it is a scientific institution with a high reputation for research. It has approximately 10,000 students, about 34% of whom are postgraduates. The second university I shall call University B. This is a university with about 8,000 full-time students, which was granted University College status in 1922 and full University status in 1955. It is located in, or more accurately overlooking, a cathedral town in the West Country.

7.5 Analysis of Prospectus A

This prospectus comes in two parts. The first is a conventional glossy book for entry in 2000, with all departments entered in alphabetical order, including the entry for the Department of Computing. This I call the 'main prospectus'. The second is a glossy, nine-page,

FRANCES GRUNDY

A4 booklet (undated) on undergraduate courses offered by the Department of Computing; I call this the 'booklet'.

7.5.1 Undergraduate Degree Programmes

There is a range of degrees offered, some of 4-years' duration (Master of Engineering [MEng] or Master of Science [MSci]), and some of 3-years' duration (Bachelor of Engineering [BEng] or Bachelor of Science [BSc]). All the degrees in computing are either BEng or MEng and are collected under the heading 'Computer Integrated Engineering Study Scheme': Computing, Computing (Mathematical Foundations), Computing (AI), Computing (Software Engineering), Computing (Computational Management), Computing (European Programme of Study). These are taught almost entirely by the Department of Computing. The degrees in Information Systems Engineering (BEng and MEng) are taught jointly by the Department of Computing and the Department of Electrical and Electronic Engineering. The only BSc and MSci degrees on offer are Mathematics and Computer Science, and these are taught jointly by the Departments of Mathematics and Computing. The total expected intake in the current year (1999-2000) is 160, which is high by old university standards, although, of course, readers of the prospectus may not know that. The proportion of women undergraduates in the department is not in the prospectus, but I was given the information over the telephone by a member of the department's clerical/administrative staff that the intake for 1998–1999 was 118, of which 11 (or 9%) were female (July, 1999).

'Bachelors' or 'Masters' degrees are masculine titles, as they are in all subject areas. The subject area in the full titles of the degrees is engineering or science. As is almost invariably the case, these titles mirror the location of this computing department in the University's academic structure – a location that is to be found in most universities. These titles are all redolent of no-nonsense, down-to-earth, 'hard' courses as distinct from liberal arts or social

122

science courses. As such, they carry the message that I suggested earlier that these are subject areas into which women are likely to find it difficult to assimilate (Camp 1997; Henwood 1996; Tonso 1999; Wolffensperger 1993)

7.5.2 Introduction to the Subject of 'Computing'

The introduction in the main prospectus is written by the male admissions tutor (the reader will know he is male because a small portrait photograph appears on the same page). It starts with questions. The first paragraph reads

> How do we understand, reason, plan, cooperate, converse, read and communicate? What are the roles of language and logic? What is the structure of the brain? How does vision work? These are questions as fundamental in their way as questions about the sub-atomic structure of matter. They are also questions where the science of computing plays an important role in our attempts to provide answers. The computer scientist can expect to come face-to-face with problems of great depth and complexity and, together with scientists, engineers and experts in other fields, may help to disentangle them. But computing is not just about the big questions it is also about 'engineering' — making things work. Computing is unique in offering both the challenge of science and the satisfaction of engineering.

This introduction starts with exciting questions implying that the computer scientist plays an important role in trying to answer these questions. I have argued elsewhere that computing is not a science though, like mathematics, it is an important facilitator of science and produces tools that scientists in other disciplines can use. So the phrase "important role" is misleading – the role may be important, but it is not scientific in the traditional sense. This sleight of hand – which makes a tool become a science – is a commonly used manoeuvre in computing circles. Having completed this manoeuvre, the author then makes the firm and solid suggestion that the successful student will now become a member of this group. "The computer scientist can now come face to face with problems of great depth and complexity." And then in the next sentence, the student is told that "computing" not computer science any more, is about engineering, and so the student can become an "engineer" as well. But note that in doing so he or she will no longer be involved in the "big" questions – they are the business of scientists not engineers.

When one looks at the degree programs more closely, computer science does not figure all that prominently. It appears in the Mathematical Foundations version of the computing degree and in the Mathematics and Computer Science degree course. This implies that in practice, and in spite of what is suggested in the admissions tutor's introduction, the science of 'computer science' is only to be found in the mathematical components of the subject. I have already noted that a BSc or MSci is only attainable in the Mathematics and Computer Science variants.

7.5.3 Departmental Self-Image

In the main prospectus, immediately after the admission tutor's introduction, there is a heading, "Computing at University A". The first paragraph says that this is one of the United Kingdom's largest computing departments and a world research leader in computer science and software engineering; the booklet confirms that this is one of the United Kingdom's largest computing departments. As both documents point out, size ensures that subjects are taught by specialists. But the student is also left to assume that being in a large department, which is a world leader in research, will give them the education they want – this is a huge step. In fact, the department has been rated "excellent", and this is mentioned in the main prospectus, but it doesn't say the rating is for teaching, although the context implies that this is the case.[11] In the booklet, too, the department is called "A world leader in teaching and research", although there is no indication of where they acquired the accolade of "*world* leader".

On equipment, it is said that "The Department traditionally provides student computing facilities which are amongst the best in the United Kingdom." The booklet says "the size of the department ensures that the variety and sophistication of equipment and specialised technical support available are of the highest order." There are two further 'large steps' here. The first is that the size of a department does ensure that the variety and sophistication of equipment and specialized technical support *are* available. To suppose that this equipment will benefit undergraduates (which the prospectus seems to imply) is another large step for any but the most self-assertive.

Self-assertion in this context, where the scene is already set by the fact that it is 'masculine' subjects that are being presented, can be perceived as overbearing and is not an encouragement to the majority of women.

The presentation of computing resources

In the main prospectus, under the section heading "Computing facilities for students", there are five subsections describing laboratories and clusters of equipment. These subsections are written mostly with the resources as the main subject of each sentence, apart from two sentences in which "students" appears as the main subject. Nowhere does it say "You [the student] have these resources available to you."

The department describes itself as having the following teaching facilities:

... PC workstations plus a number of other systems. The PCs are configured to run Microsoft's Windows NT 4.0 and RedHat Linux 5.1 operating systems, have 17-inch colour monitors, sound cards and fast ethernet working. There are several 300MHz Pentium II machines, with 128 Mb and 3-dimensional graphics hardware, forming the latest phase of our rolling upgrade programme. Software available for use in the laboratory includes: Microsoft Office Professional '97 (word processing, spreadsheets, databases), Visual Studio 5.0 (C, C++ and Java), Mathematica, the Xilinx VLSI design system, Turing, Sicstus Prolog, Haskell and Netscape Communicator ...

The workstations are supported by a Compaq Proliant 1600R fileserver with 172GB disk space (called hex) and 2 dual processor 512 Mb computer servers (pingu and pinga), connected by fast ethernet and Extreme Network's gigabit backbone switches.

This extraordinary catalogue reflects not just the fact that computing requires the use of hardware, but that technological devices are an important source of power for men and help to provide an environment in which they can bond together and maintain a centre of power (see, for example Cockburn (Cockburn 1988)). Potential male recruits will already have an inkling of the value of computer hardware for conferring status. The greater the power, the speed, and the 'up-to-datedness' of the hardware, the better. And this applies to software, too. So the presentation of hardware and software through the medium of these prospectuses can be used to foster this use of computers as a source of power and ensure that it is reproduced in the next generation.

One wonders whether in writing the prospectus in this way the authors are aware that young men are more likely to be *au fait* with recent hardware and software than young women and that the parading of such awesome computer power is probably more likely to daunt than dazzle many women. Young men, on the other hand, will probably be attracted by it. It could be that this assertion underestimates modern young women. However, my anecdotal experience as well as that of colleagues is that this kind of labelling of equipment is off-putting and indeed, on occasions, frightening to women. It is a topic worthy of further research.

In the booklet, computing equipment is presented on page 4, before detailed information about undergraduate courses. The word 'laboratory' is used for all the rooms that house computers. This word has long been widely used in universities to describe the rooms containing computer terminals, workstations, and so on, where students practice their computing. 'Laboratory' connotes scientific experiments and the use of scientific equipment to test and measure results. Just how off-putting this term is to women we don't know. All that can be said is, if the 'scientific' framework does make the subject unattractive to women, the use of this word is bound to contribute to its deterrent effect.[12]

Although students and their assignments are mentioned twice, the descriptions of the equipment are again impersonal. It is the hardware and the software that are the main subjects. All of this emphasizes that computing in this institution is not focused on people but on equipment and research. For example,

> "Word processing and simple computer graphics are also carried out... Programs may be developed in Pascal ..."

The power and speed of the hardware are emphasized by such phrases as "powerful Sun Sparc files servers" and "high speed ATM ..." and some machines labelled "supercomputers" are described as providing "state-of-the-art parallel computing facilities to groups doing research needing supercomputer power."

FRANCES GRUNDY

The role of research

Research activity is presented in the booklet on page 3, and in considerable detail. Even the four, male, professorial heads of research sections are named. This appears before presentation of any information on undergraduate courses, which is primarily what the reader is looking for. This presentation of research activity, before anything of substance on undergraduate courses, contributes to the prevailing philosophy that research in university departments comes before teaching. This impression is confirmed by statements such as, "We are proud of our department, not just of its resources and teaching, but also of its students." This ordering establishes for the undergraduates, before they have even applied, the primacy of research.

Even the supercomputers are special equipment purchased for the use of highly valued researchers. The final sentence of the section on this equipment says, "Students doing individual projects may be granted access to these facilities by their supervisors". The position of research in the power structure is again being clearly stated, and students are being encouraged to value access to this equipment.

It may well be that the more prestigious of the old universities need, in a highly competitive situation, to emphasize their strength in the crucial area of research, and, of course, listing an impressive array of research hardware is one way of doing this.

On the face of it, people will be attracted by this glittering array of research activities and associated equipment. Being at the 'cutting edge' and at the forefront of scientific research is a factor that assists in giving science much of its kudos. After all, the 'purest' and most prestigious scientists are the research scientists.[13] Such vaunting of its research record by a 'science' department and the consequent enhancement of its 'scientific' image may attract more men but may not have a positive or even a neutral effect on women – indeed it may put them off. One consequence is that the prospectus may continue to attract male applicants at the expense of remaining unattractive to women. To ensure that these prospectuses do attract women, this image of research and its impact on prospective undergraduate students of both genders must itself be investigated.

There has, for some years now, been more effort to raise the standing of teaching in rating institutions and staff (see endnote [11] for example), but this has not really changed the relative weightings of teaching and research. Research still has much financial clout.

Emphasis on 'up-to-datedness'

I have already noted the use of 'the latest' hardware as a device for male dominance and that this valuation extends to software. I would now extend it to computing techniques. This theme of 'up-to-datedness' permeates both documents.

In the main prospectus we have, "Constant updating of knowledge is essential" (p. 89); "constantly updated optional courses" (p. 90); "Courses are constantly being revised and updated" (p. 92); "development of state-of-the-art applications and technologies" (p. 95); "The latest Field Programmable Gate Array Technology . . . " (p.101); "state-of-the-art parallel computing facilities" (p. 102). And in the booklet we have, "The Department's computer facilities are constantly updated in line with the latest advances in technology . . . magnificent new 128-processor AP1000 parallel supercomputer is being donated to the College by Fujitsu" (p.4).

7.5.4 Use of the First and Second or the Third Person

With the exception of the entries for the Careers, and Health and Welfare Services, the third person is used in the general introduction to the main prospectus, the department's entry in the main prospectus, and in the booklet. There is one instance of the use of "we" in the department's entry in the main prospectus, which I have mentioned above. The subjects of sentences are typically, as well as the names of hardware and software, "MEng students", "BEng students", "The course", "Applicants", "The Department of Computing", etc. It is never "You".

7.5.5 Any Specific Encouragement for Women to Apply?

In the general introduction of the main prospectus there is the tangential statement, "Our women students make a great contribution to College life; there have been seven women presidents of the Students' Union in recent years". And later, "At present 31 per cent of our students are women and there are ever-widening career opportunities for women science and engineering graduates." Two-day WISE (Women into Science and Engineering) courses are offered in the summer.

In the introduction to the departmental entry all that it says is, "There are fewer barriers of age and sex, and the industry is leading the way in flexible working practices and career planning." It does not say what proportion of undergraduates in the department are female. In fact, the figure of 9% that I was given compares unfavourably with the University-wide figure just given. There are no specific invitations to women to apply for computing courses. So women students are mentioned only obliquely.

7.5.6 Photographs and Illustrations (Excluding Alumni)

In the main prospectus there is one photograph of the male admissions tutor beside the introductory statement about the subject, which I have already mentioned. Only one woman appears in the two photographs of students working with computing equipment (I call these 'working group pictures', which does not imply that students are working together; in fact, in only two of all these photos are students seen working together).

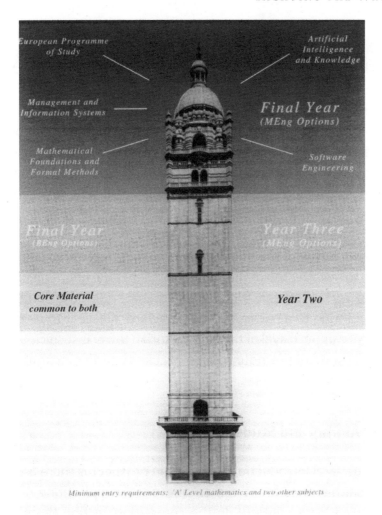

European Programme of Study

Artificial Intelligence and Knowledge

Management and Information Systems

Final Year (MEng Options)

Mathematical Foundations and Formal Methods

Software Engineering

Final Year (MEng Options)

Year Three (MEng Options)

Core Material common to both

Year Two

Minimum entry requirements: 'A' Level mathematics and two other subjects

Figure 7.1: *Victorian tower – Prospectus A*

In the booklet there are four working group pictures with apparently no women in any of them. On the cover there are two leisure pictures (pictures of students engaged in social activities); one includes a woman with her face partly hidden by a glass, although equally 1 of the 2 men's faces is turned away almost entirely from the camera, and in the foreground of the other picture there are 1 woman and 6 men. These all seem to hint at the proportions of women in the department. So, all in all there are 3 women and 34 men, which makes women 8% of the total – less than the 9% given for the current year.

This institution has on its campus a tall, prominent Victorian tower built in white stone with a green copper domed top. It is a landmark in the locality, and a postcard-type photograph taken from street level appears in colour on the front of the booklet. Inside the booklet this is used in a full-page illustration showing how each of the various degrees on offer is obtained year by year as one 'moves up' the tower (Fig 7.1). Because it is a symbolic representation, it appears starkly in black and white and without any of the surrounding buildings. The background is blue – light blue at the bottom with the colour becoming more intense as one moves up the tower. The top of the tower represents the final year of study for the 4-year courses. White lines emanate from the domed top, each pointing to a particular degree award. I leave it to readers to decide if this portrayal of this fine Victorian tower is suspiciously like a phallic symbol promoting the masculinity of the institution and these computing courses.

7.5.1 Alumni and Student Profile

In the general introduction to the main prospectus there are short personal histories for two men and one woman (none of these graduated in computing). In the computing section there is one personal history of a man – a current student. In the computing section of the 1999 prospectus there was a personal history of a woman, then a current student, who appeared in a photograph working at a computer and looking confident and conventionally glamorous. She was not by any means a woman with whom the majority of women would identify. Why show a picture of a woman who is attractive to conventional heterosexual men? One wonders if it was in fact the department showing prospective male students what type of women this prestigious institution can attract regardless of what deterrent effects showing such confident women might have on those women lacking in confidence. Again, research into the effects of this type of picture on both women and men would be informative.

7.6 Analysis of Prospectus B

This prospectus also had two parts. The first, which again I call the 'main prospectus', is a conventional glossy book for entry in 2000, with the schools of the University entered in alphabetical order; the Department of Computer Science appears under the entry for the School of Engineering and Computer Science. The second document is an undated departmental booklet of 13 pages. It seems to be 'home produced' (this is not a criticism), with few special features to attract attention. These were also accompanied by an A4, one-page leaflet. Since this carried no extra information, I shall not refer to it.

7.6.1 Undergraduate Degree Programs

The range of degree programs is much narrower than that at University A: a 3-year BSc in Computer Science and a 3-year interdisciplinary BSc in Cognitive Science run jointly by the Department of Computer Science and the School of Psychology. There are also 'Major/Minor' degrees, where the major subject is Computer Science and the minor subjects are Mathematical Studies (3-years) and European Study (4-years). The booklet is only concerned with the degrees involving Computer Science.

In reply to an e-mail request, the percentage of women in the 1998–1999 intake for all these courses was given as 14.3 (Tracy Darroch, 30 July 1999). However, the figure for the Cognitive Science degree taken alone was 43.7%. Psychology traditionally has a very high percentage of females; for example, the 1998–1999 intake of women at my own University was 78%, so if we remove the Cognitive Science data, the figure for the other degrees is 6.6%.

7.6.2 Departmental Self-Image

The opening paragraph of the department's entry in the main prospectus reads

> The Department has 20 academic and support staff and caters for an annual intake of about 65 students. This creates an attractive environment where staff and students work together in a friendly and informal atmosphere. We have a broad interest in software development spanning parallel computing, multimedia systems, neural computing, visualisation and artificial intelligence. Student placements and research collaborations give us a wide range of contacts with commercial and industrial companies.

The opening emphasis here is on friendship and cooperation in work; this department is in fact one of the smaller university computing departments in the country, although all readers of the prospectus might not know this. The list of interests is not presented here as research interests but, by implication, teaching interests, although it could be research interests as well. It is an undergraduate prospectus, and it is written as if it were just that.

The next paragraph describes computing equipment:

> We provide a network of Pentium PCs running both Unix and Windows operating systems. For more specialist work we have a cluster of Silicon Graphics multimedia workstations. You may use these facilities from our laboratories which have 24-hour access.

Unlike the equivalent University A entry, which is long, technical, and meant to dazzle, and in which the word "you" never appears, this describes computing equipment from a teaching and learning point of view.

The third paragraph of this introduction starts, "You will be involved in a variety of learning environments ...". The pronouns "you" and "we", and the corresponding possessive pronouns, are used extensively throughout the entry for Computer Science and indeed throughout the whole prospectus. As David Lee (Lee 1992, p. 122) points out, quoting a summary of findings of cross-gender conversations, "Women tend to acknowledge the addressee with more frequent use of the pronouns *you* and *we*."

The booklet opens in a similar welcoming vein and states that the department has been rated "excellent" in teaching.[12] Unlike the main prospectus, the list of departmental interests in the introductory page is called "research interests".

7.6.3 Introduction to the Subject of 'Computer Science'

There is no attempt to discuss why the title 'Computer Science' is used. The emphasis is on what skills the subject requires: "Computer Science ... demand[s] a blend of creativity and technical skills" ... "you will study the theoretical foundations of computer science." Partly because there are no degrees offered in computer or software engineering, the word 'engineering' is notable for its near absence in both documents. It is, of course, in the title of the School and, apart from that, appears in 'software engineering' in the list of modules.

Under the heading "Aims of the Degree Programmes", the Computer Science program is presented as centred on what students can gain from the course and, to a certain extent, what they can bring to it.

> ... You will be encouraged to debate and reflect on the effects of [new] developments on society and on individual lifestyles.
>
> Computer technology does not stand still. So, as a student of computer science, your aim will be to

> acquire the necessary intellectual, practical and personal skills to adapt readily to future changes. Our aim is to provide degree programmes which foster these adaptive skills.

Unlike the prospectus for University A, there is no large gap between the department's description of itself and its computer science course, on the one hand, and the education students are looking for, on the other. And although both departments recognize that things are moving fast, and students will need the skills to keep up with changes, the tone from University B is less demanding and more facilitating than that from A.

7.6.4 Research Profile

There is no explicit mention of staff research interests or of research programs in the main prospectus, though the second sentence of the opening paragraph quoted above, which starts, "We have a broad interest in . . ." strongly hints that research is happening. But from the point of view of this document, one of the main functions of research appears to be to support and underpin undergraduate teaching.

In the booklet, the research interests of the department are listed in one sentence, and elsewhere it states that 3rd-year options will be determined by the research interests of the department. To some extent, these statements detract from the more teaching centredness of much of the rest of the texts.

7.6.5 Presentation of Computing Resources

I have already quoted the short paragraph in the departmental introduction of the main prospectus which describes the hardware available for students to use and includes the word 'laboratories'.

In the booklet, the computing resources are presented under

the heading *Facilities*. The type of machines available are named and proprietary names are given for software, but the list is not long. The word 'laboratories' is not used.

7.6.6 Encouragement to Women to Apply?

There is no mention of attracting women either in the general introduction of the main prospectus or in the department's entry in the main prospectus. So, in this respect this main prospectus is even less encouraging of women than that of University A. The proportion of women undergraduates in the department is not given.

In the booklet, a section entitled "Your questions answered" contains 11 questions; the 10th of these is, "Are your degrees attractive to female students?" The answer is

"Yes, and their excellent results prove it. Of particular interest has been our user-centred approach to systems development and emphasis on development of personal skills."

7.6.7 Photographs and Student Profile

The department's entry in the main prospectus has four photographs: one of these is of 2 students, 1 male and 1 female, video conferencing one another. There is a photograph of 2 men in the staff/student common room. To have a common room for both staff and (presumably) undergraduate students is rare in computing departments. So, this caption harks back to the opening paragraph, which talks about staff and students working together in a friendly environment. But to assume that common rooms are free from power politics and, in particular gendered-power politics, is naïve. "Most formal and informal meetings – at home, socially and in work organisations involve some degree of power acknowledgement and response" (Nicolson 1996, pp. 66–67). And Nicolson continues, "Some individuals walk away from struggles for power, particularly if they know they will not win" (see also (Grundy 1996, p. 50)). To presume that undergraduate women would not have problems with such common rooms seems unrealistic. Moreover, it is hardly encouraging to women that the only people shown using it are men. The third picture is part of the profile of a male student. The fourth is of some people engaged in joint group work in which a man is speaking to the group; the gender of the others in the photograph is not completely clear but they are most probably 3 women and 2 men.

There is one 'pastiche' of colour photographs and a drawing occupying the front cover of the booklet, which has a mix of men and women at work (none engaged in computing) and at 'play'. So, all in all there are 9 men and 7 women, making women 44% of the total.

There is one personal history in the computer science section of the main prospectus – that of a man in his 3rd year.

7.7 Discussion

7.7.1 Computer 'Science' and Computer 'Engineering'

My suggestion is that the masculine connotations of science and engineering that have been carried over into computing are evident in these prospectuses and, more controversially, that they contribute to the general disinclination of women to enter the subject. The words 'science' and 'engineering' are, of course, present in the titles of degrees, departments, faculties, and schools and, in the case of engineering, in modules or courses. The science component, although present, is less and less obvious now; however, we have seen that one department does seek to use this connection in its initial invitation to attract students. But the over-arching presence of the word contributes to the awesome image that computing has for most women and that some men find challenging and attractive. The institution that is the more aggressive in selling itself, University A, is the one that uses the word 'science' to sell its computing to prospective undergraduates; it is implicitly at the 'frontiers of science'.

This is also the one university of the two that has written more about hardware and which has named more items of hardware and software. It is the one that has given a far higher profile to its research programs, which are not of immediate interest to prospective undergraduates and are possibly of interest to fewer women than men.

The use of the first and second as opposed to the third person gives a greater sense of connection, which women tend to seek more than men (Gilligan 1993). It is noticeable that the third person is used almost exclusively in prospectus A whereas this is not the case in prospectus B.

7.1.2 Specific Encouragement to Women

It seems significant that, despite the very low recruitment levels of women into these courses, there is hardly any attempt in either of these prospectuses to persuade women to take up computing. Maybe the reason for this is the belief that to describe courses as suitable for women would deter lots of men. By encouraging women one would merely change the proportions of women to men, leaving the overall numbers of students much the same. Rather than do this both departments have, in common with most others, opted for the *status quo*. They may not have consciously opted for it, but their implicit value judgement is nonetheless that it is more valuable to maintain the number of men than to recruit more women. There can be no justification for such a decision. In fact, to increase the number of women – even at the expense of the number of men – is, given the existing low numbers of women, on the balance of probability likely to improve the overall standard of students. In other words, assuming that, in general terms, women and men are of equal ability in computing, to maximize the average ability of the intake means that women and men have to be recruited in equal numbers.[14].

7.7.3 What Else Is Needed?

The assumption in the last paragraph is that specific invitations to women will attract them in greater numbers. This assumption needs testing. It could be that the apparent neutrality of the prospectuses from the new universities, which I chose not to analyse, is more attractive to women than specific invitations, because women who read these prospectuses fear that they are being inveigled into 'a hotbed of feminism'. On the other hand, if more institutions were explicit in their invitations, they wouldn't be perceived as extreme.

Space precluded the detailed examination of more than two prospectuses. Further prospectuses should be analysed, particularly those from new universities in the United Kingdom. (The fact that they are not research oriented to the extent that the old universities are should be taken into account.) The analysis of prospectuses, where they exist, from other 'Western' and 'non-Western' countries would be interesting, too.

In fact, at several points in this chapter I have made assertions that need research. One such assumption concerns the possible differential effects on potential female and male undergraduates of the highlighting of research activities and associated hardware in these prospectuses. Another presumption I have been making and that ought to be researched is that those women who lack confidence in their ability are deterred by self-assertive institutions and are more encouraged by ones that do not exhibit such traits.

Above all, perhaps, there should be research into the role of the science/engineering paradigm, the way women react to lists of hardware and software, and to the emphasis on 'having the latest'.

The analysis of the photographs would benefit from more detailed study. The working photographs in both sets of prospectuses all show students working at computers, that is, working with the hardware. This is conventional in this context nowadays. In the case of University B, there is an instance of people using hardware to communicate with one another. But involvement with other people at work and the use of computers to assist in that is largely absent in both prospectuses. Both prospectuses show more men than women in their photographs. The value of role models in these photographs is not explicit. More research needs to be done to determine what type of women should be shown and what activities they should be engaged in to attract more women to the computing field.

But before all that, those commissioning these prospectuses must find the will to target women more than men.

PART IV
CHANGE?

CHAPTER 8

TIME IN THE GENDER-TECHNOLOGY RELATIONSHIP

Presented as Keynote address at ITechWomen International
Conference, Vienna City Hall, 22–23 October 2001

Abstract

FOR ALL THE SPEED of change that is taking place, particularly in IT, it does not seem that women's position is improving much – if at all. The figures for female employment in this industry are not encouraging; indeed in the US the percentage is falling. However, two recent surveys from the US suggest that women in hi-tech industries are exhilarated and excited by this work; they are confident in their intellectual capability to keep up with change. But they are also exhausted. Their addiction to 'faster, smarter, newer' is leading to long hours and are causing many of these women to consider leaving their jobs. They cannot achieve what they feel is important to them, namely a work/life balance. That is to say, they feel they do not have enough time for their families, let alone for wider relationships outside the family. One thing which might help is less emphasis on the 'faster, smarter, newer' and tolerance of older approaches and techniques together with a pluralism that places less emphasis on there being only one right way of doing things. On the domestic front, in spite of much rhetoric there has been almost no change in who bears the major part of these responsibilities. According to one of these surveys both men and women agree that domestic technology, telecommuting and so on have helped, but the fact remains that women still bear the burden. One obvious element in the resolution of this is for women to do what so many of them have been urging for so long: let men take up their rightful share of domestic duties.

8.1 Introduction

Towards the conclusion of *A Room of One's Own* Virginia Woolf writes

> Here then, Mary Beton ceases to speak [Mary Beton was a pseudonym Woolf adopted for this essay]. She has told you how she reached the conclusion – the prosaic conclusion – that it is necessary to have five hundred a year and a room with a lock on the door if you are to write fiction or poetry. (Woolf 1993)

Here Woolf, writing in 1928, identifies two material factors without which women are unlikely to be able to write; sufficient money to live on and privacy – time by oneself to do what one wants to do. She quotes Florence Nightingale "women never have half an hour . . . they can call their own" (p. 60).[15]And this in spite of the fact that Woolf was well-to-do, had no children and had not burdened herself with household duties; like many women in her circumstances she had others to do her household chores. I want to show how this need for privacy and attitude to time contrasts interestingly with what women involved with technology want nowadays, which is much more complex and paradoxical than it was for Virginia Woolf. For those of us now involved with technology, and for others too, lack of time is a huge issue.

It wasn't only Virginia Woolf who prompted me to write about time. In 1997, my friend and colleague Eva Turner (Turner 1997) wrote about an inaugural lecture she attended (this is a lecture given by newly appointed professors in British universities). A new research professor in the Faculty of Technology was, following a welcome to his family, being applauded for all he had achieved by the time he was aged about 40. It was indeed remarkable; at one time the youngest professor of computer science, he published 3 books and 80 peer-reviewed papers in distinguished journals, wrote 210 other articles, made appearances on television and radio and so on. Observing his wife and four young children in the audience, Eva speculated what his wife could have achieved in the world of paid work had she wanted to. As it was, the occasion was a public endorsement of a man being able to further his career at the expense of his wife not having a career because she was looking after children and home. Insult was added to injury in that his family was one of *his* achievements. It was a public endorsement of the fact that it is admissible to have an unpaid person on hand and unacknowledged, in any real sense, to enable this man to collapse the time needed for one important aspect of his life to zero while making it look as if he had spent time on it.

This is a story we have all seen repeated and the issues involved in this distribution of opportunities are still of the greatest importance. What I want to do in this paper is to give a kind of progress report on the present gender-technology-time relationship. I shall argue that such a report must come to a very mixed conclusion. There are things to welcome and applaud. On the other hand, there are areas where there has been stunningly little progress. This might help identify some of the facets of these relationships which need attention.

I mentioned my own discipline and I shall continue to use that to illustrate the points I am making.

8.2 The Time Paradox

It is a truism that technological change is accelerating at a dizzying rate and this is nowhere more true than in the case of my own discipline, computing. Gordon Moore got it right in 1965 when he predicted that the number of transistors per square inch on integrated circuits would continue to double every year for the foreseeable future. This observation is, of course, what became known as Moore's law. We are always hearing figures describing the rate of increase of the use of the Internet, and we are all well aware of the growth in the use of computers. So one might, on the face of it, have hoped that the position of women in these fast moving technologies would improve. Unfortunately, however, it is also a truism that the position of women in most of these technologies is very slow to change.

In 1999 the employment of women in the IT workforce in the US was 29% compared to 47% in the overall workforce. This figure for employment in IT represents a drop from 40% in 1986 (Council of Economic Advisers 2000). And a further press report from the US suggests that in 2000 the figure for women in the IT workforce was 20% and that "computer science is actually one of the few job groups where the percentage of women in the industry is decreasing, according to the Department of Labor, in Washington DC" (Datamation 2000). And, in the UK, a figure of 16% is quoted by the Equal Opportunities Commission (EOC 2002). This represents a drop from 19% for 2000 (EOC 2001). Another comparable figure quoted in the British press in 2001 was 23% (Computing 2001) . And in India the figure is 15% (Gupta 2001). Given the speed at which technology changes, these figures suggest a change occurring at a disappointingly slow pace for women.

In spite of these figures, developments are taking place that point to a much more complex and not so unrelievedly gloomy story. As we shall see, these developments raise, in a new setting, the old discussions amongst feminists about the definitions of work and leisure. They also raise interesting questions about the speed of change and our general uncritical acceptance of this phenomenon in the world of IT. On the one hand one cannot deny that these changes are exciting, on the other hand, what's feeding us is choking us. The phenomenon has both advantages and disadvantages – upsides and downsides. The same features that provide great job satisfaction are producing stress and a feeling of not being able to balance work and life.

8.2.1 In the USA

Let's start with the good news. The recruitment of women into hi-tech companies in the US is excellent; according to one estimate, 55% of the people recruited into these companies are women (Computerworld 2001). Furthermore, according to two reports of surveys of the hi-tech industry in the US (I shall confine my observations to the US because of the availability of data) women are really enjoying themselves.

The first of these reports is of a survey of 265 women members of an organisation called WorldWIT (Gewirtz & Lindsey 2015).

Another report that I shall call the 'Roper report', conducted and published in 2001, interviewed 1000 women and 500 men who use AOL at least once a day. Some classified themselves as online professionals, others not (Roper 2001). While this survey identifies women's excitement with the new industry, it also reveals that many women are not entirely happy with their situation. The Roper survey was of both men and women and does not seek out the reasons why women in particular want to leave in the same open way that the Gewirtz & Lindsey survey does.

8.2.2 Upsides and Downsides

The women expressed both positive and negative points or, as I have called them here, 'upsides' and 'downsides'. Here first are some of the upsides.

- 3% of women spoke about their ability to have an impact, a sense of satisfaction, achievement, autonomy, and freedom to be creative. They experienced fewer gender-related issues, though they still exist. (G & L, p. 3)
- "It's exciting to be on the cutting edge where all issues need to be rethought and nothing can be taken for granted." (G & L, p. 9)
- "The feeling of being in something big or important from the beginning is exciting. In 'old economy' jobs, women enter into something already established with expectations historically crafted around men. In the new economy, women can be involved from the foundation on up, helping craft the standards and expectations that will define the industry. It's incredibly exciting." (G & L, p. 9)
- Contrary to the well-worn idea that women lack confidence, this survey finds that women are slightly more likely than men to say they are 'very confident' in their ability to keep pace with new technology. (Roper 2001, p. 13)
- But what is exhilarating can also be exhausting.
- Only 29% of women agreed that women receive equal pay. (Roper 2001, p. 31)
- For many women the glass ceiling is still very much in place. "From the perspective of most in the high-technology industry, the glass ceiling is an impediment to advancing." (Roper 2001, p. 34)
- Working long hours is the norm according to 68% of all hi-tech professionals (women and men) (Roper 2001, p. 22)
- Some women feel they are expected to fit it all in, their work in the new economy, their personal community and family life and they feel they can't. This generates lots of stress, as one woman put it "The stupid Internet time". (G & L, p. 10)
- Some women think that the pressure of time is bad for their families. One woman said she feels that "mothers in the workforce are the most discriminated against of any

category going". One senior woman simply said "Frankly, I tend not to hire people with young families". (G & L, p. 14)

- Stress and anxiety are common. 56% of women experience moderate or high stress and anxiety regarding the instability of their company's market. 59% felt it regarding the intensity of demands placed on them at work and for 67% of women it was the rapid pace of change that brought this experience of high stress/anxiety. (G & L, p. 19)

8.2.3 Time and Autonomy

One of the things that emerges most strongly and clearly from the Gewirtz & Lindsey report is the way women in high-technology value their time which they regard as "precious". In consequence, they also value highly their autonomy to use that time as they think fit. One of the things they feel most strongly is the benefits accruing when the old masculine hierarchies are removed and a new system is put in its place. Or, to put it the other way around, they would resent giving up their time to working in old masculine hierarchies.

All this gives a lot of flexibility in the use of one's time to achieve goals and indeed the time to determine what those goals should be.

"You are your own boss. You make the decisions and get to implement without spending lots of time working with bureaucracy . . . The ups are much greater – because you feel the impact of your contributions." (G & L, p. 8).

I should add in passing that there are also findings from the UK that there is counter evidence that these collaborative systems are working, partly I suspect because in the instances cited, they are being introduced in the wrong context (Woodfield 2000).

And yet, both the reports I have cited indicate that many women are unhappy with their work.

"41% of women were thinking of leaving or have recently looked at other job opportunities, but were staying" (G & L, p. 25).

60% of women (compared with 45% of men) said that if they

were starting again they would not choose the high-technology industry (Roper 2001).

8.2.4 Work/Life Balance

Judging by the complaints these women make about the amount of time they have to spend at work, they are finding considerable difficulty in striking a balance between work and their family/ community and, indeed, themselves. A lot of women, in particular those who are mothers, find that striking this work/life balance is very difficult, if not impossible.

Gewirtz & Lindsey hypothesise that the high numbers considering leaving the industry may, in part, be due to stress or work/life balance issues.

"No life besides work" (p. 10)

"For women the expectation [is] that you can juggle it all – personal, home, office, and the reality is you can't." (p. 11)

A significant proportion of women do not see a sharp contrast and opposition between time spent at work and time spent on social life as if one were the negation of the other. But in a dialectical fashion they want to synthesise the two and find that a blending rather than a balance between them is the solution.

"The personal relationships that grow out of the frenetic environment are great. Work is, for better or worse, a replacement for neighborhood communities these days." (p. 8)

"Lots of camaraderie." (p. 8)

"I network a lot with other women. We talk about running a business, marketing strategies, and our anxieties. I also try to mentor other women whenever I can – sharing my own experiences, contact, and knowledge." (p. 20)

These women, though relatively few in number, are challenging the traditional dichotomy between work and life; something I shall be returning to shortly.

8.3 Easing the Load?

8.3.1 'Up-to-datedness' and Linear Development

Amongst all the sources of stress, the pace of constant change figures very strongly (much more strongly than is suggested just by the idea of 'life-long learning'). This is in spite of the confidence expressed by these women in the hi-tech industry in their intellectual ability to keep up with developments. The technical side of IT is no problem; it is the time it takes to keep up-to-date that brings the stress.

Liisa von Hellens and Sue Nielsen (von Hellens & Nielsen 2001) report something similar emerging from their survey of women working in Australia in IT.

> One successful systems engineer said she would not encourage her young daughter to enter IT, citing the pace of the work and the need to continuously update one's personal IT knowledge and skills as incompatible with family life. (p. 15)

It is not clear to what extent the sheer increase in volume of work is a source of stress, but clearly the need to constantly update one's knowledge is one major source. I wonder if some of this striving for up-to-datedness is not misguided and perhaps women and men are adding a great deal of unnecessary stress to their lives.

The university prospectuses examined in the previous chapter provide a key to the way in which the importance of up-to-datedness manifests itself. They are, as we have seen, documents used in some countries to attract good students to the university that issues them. Whether or not they paint an attractive picture for prospective students, they are certainly very revealing of the attitudes of staff. In one of these prospectuses from a UK university there was an extraordinary list of equipment (how much it would mean to a prospective undergraduate is not clear), but in spite of this it was clearly intended to impress such readers.

One can imagine the derision in a department of the kind I have just described if one wanted to reuse software that had been 'superseded' by something more state-of-the-art. This phenomenon manifests itself in what, as I have suggested elsewhere, is something like linear development in computing (see Section 3.2.3 which questions if computing is a science).

This linear development is an echo of the way in which traditional science is said to develop. The later versions of explanations and theories are superior in truth to the earlier versions. The usual example given is the replacement of Ptolemy's planetary system by that of Copernicus. In both science and computing, the old, if not taken up into the new, is abandoned. The history of Artificial Intelligence (AI) since its inception provides an example of this (Whitby 1996). The proponents of each new generation of AI research in turn produce so much 'hype' and promise so much from their research in order to get funding that when it fails, even partially, and the next generation are seeking their funds, they label their predecessors efforts as 'failures' and then they too make promises they cannot fulfil. So each new wave of research is outmoded, is abandoned and seems, *prima facie*, past it. The new fashion then takes its place. This ambience of always 'using the latest' is found not just in AI, but generally throughout computing. Sometimes the old, if not seriously inadequate, is retained if only for economic reasons. But, on the whole, the pressure is on people to use the latest methods which have, of course, to be learned. Hence the pressure to be always up to date puts pressure on those working at the heart of computing.

The idea of linear development, including the extreme form of it found in the demands for having the very latest, gives men in computing a powerful advantage career-wise. Take, for example, a woman returner, that is one who has left the profession temporarily, perhaps to spend five or so years child rearing. She is likely to hesitate, knowing beforehand the rate at which hardware, software and techniques all change and that it's unlikely she will be given the time and money needed to catch up. Moreover, she knows she will risk being ridiculed for being 'out-of-date' and hence 'out-of-touch'. Female obsolescence seems to be built in to the system as indeed is the hierarchical domination of the system by men who do not have such unfortunate choices to make.

Being up-to-date is a feature that has been very much part of IT from its masculine inception and which everyone still seems to accept. This fetish of up-to-datedness needs challenging and there should be greater tolerance of older methods. Of course, I am not suggesting that there should be no change and indeed some change is exciting, but surely we can identify areas where the speed of change could be reduced to the immediate relief of everybody. One way of doing this would be to allow the pluralism of using new and old technologies and techniques side by side when technically possible. Obviously, this will reduce to some extent the stress of having to learn new techniques all the time – and being an outcast if one fails.

8.3.2 The Other Workload

I have been talking quite a lot about the difficulty women in the hi-tech industry have in striking a work/life balance and, of course one important factor in that is the amount of time spent doing domestic work of all sorts. Let's look at the progress, or lack of it, in the area of modern domestic technology and see how much that has done to ease the load.

Rapid changes in technology in general are not necessarily paralleled by changes in domestic technology bringing swift relief to women. A large national sample collected in 1965 showed that the time the average American woman spent doing housework and caring for children was not strikingly different from the time spent by affluent housewives in 1912 (Schwarz Cowan 1983, p. 199). In one way this is a testimony to the domestic technology of the time because it made up for the loss of paid servants as well as that of unpaid relatives (mothers, unmarried daughters and sisters, children). But the fact that women in 1965 had to work the same hours as they did in 1912 is a disappointment. It is likely that domestic technology being typically designed by men for women, i.e. not by its primary users, has made it less efficient.

Developments in domestic technology are helpfully summed up by Judy Wajcman

> This change in the structure of the household labour force [the loss of servants] was accompanied by a remodelled ideology of housewifery. The development in the early years of this century of the domestic science movement, and a germ theory of disease and the idea of 'scientific motherhood', led to new exacting standards of housework and childcare. As standards of personal and household cleanliness rose during the twentieth century women were expected to produce clean toilets, bathtubs, and sinks. With the introduction of washing machines, laundering increased because of higher expectations of cleanliness. There was a major change in the importance attached to child rearing and mother's role. The average housewife had fewer children, but modern 'child-centred' approaches to parenting involved her in spending much more time and effort. These trends were exploited and further promoted by advertisers in their drive to expand the market for domestic appliances.
>
> Housework began to be presented as an expression of the housewife's affection for her family. The split between public and private meant that the home was expected to provide a haven from the alienated, stressful technological order of the workplace and

was expected to provide entertainment, emotional support, and sexual gratification. The burden of satisfying these needs fell on the housewife. (Wajcman 1991, pp. 85–86)

This was the situation until the early 1990s. Now, responses to the Roper report indicate that women (91% of them) think that the creation of time-saving devices has made women's lives better (of course we don't know what women in the 1965 survey actually thought). The demand for yet more cleanliness seems to have plateaued out; my personal observations are that women in search of, or doing, paid work are much more prepared to let some standards, those which they deem unnecessary, fall. Recent developments such as cheaper food freezers, washing machines and microwave ovens, and better quality convenience foods have also possibly contributed to time saving in domestic work. 91% of women responding to the Roper survey think that the ability to work from home (telecommuting) has had a positive effect on women's lives. 79% of women think the creation of on-line shopping has had a good effect. And, in the case of the cell-phone, 75% of women think this has had a positive effect on women's lives. Interestingly, men agreed with all these observations in almost exactly the same proportions, although always slightly less. (Roper 2001, p. 15)

So some progress has been made, but where is the systematic tackling of this problem across the whole front? It's now almost half a century since Frances GABe started work on her Self-Cleaning House (GABe 2001). The striking feature about that house to me now is, not so much the individual devices like the General Room-Washing Apparatus, the Dust Expelling Drawers and the No-Bother Containers, but the fact that she had the vision and the courage to set about tackling the whole house from foundations upwards. It was a systematic and comprehensive attack across the whole gamut of housework including the house itself. The bringing together of all that computer technology can provide with such elementary ideas as sloping floors (on adjustable joists) and dishwasher cupboards, in one real labour-saving house, just has not happened yet.

What about the fact that men agree with women in their answers to these questions? Is it that, if women's lot really is improving with all these devices, these men are now let off the hook and to answer 'yes' to these questions salves their consciences? Indeed, how come this question is still being asked? At the time of these surveys it was almost 20 years since Ruth Schwarz Cowan's book was published on this subject [16] and yet we are still asking 'has women's lot improved?' The answer is: women are still working the double shift and there are powerful forces at work which just do not care.

How do we ease women's domestic load? Not, I suggest, simply by introducing more labour-saving devices of the kind introduced so far. None of these has made the radical difference so many of us have sought for so long.

8.4 'Work/Life Balance': What does this mean?

It has long been recognised (for example, (Green et al. 1990)) that for women the boundaries between work and leisure are, as I should like to characterise them, fluid, individual and grey. By 'fluid' I mean constantly changing, by 'individual' I imply that the boundaries are different for each person and by 'grey' I mean the distinction is extremely difficult to make – even for one individual at any point in time.

I am conscious that there is a host of literature out there about work and leisure, so I shall make some somewhat naïve characterisations of these terms and shall certainly not attempt definitions. It is difficult even to give an adequate characterisation of either of these words without prejudging any issues.

'Paid work' is work that is paid for in cash or kind. 'Domestic work' is fulfilling obligations, self or societally imposed, towards the family however extended it may be. 'Additional work' is fulfilling other obligations e.g. to a church or political party. In principle, all these types of work can be pleasurable to the extent that they are so enjoyable that a person derives more enjoyment from them than from leisure activities.

For my part, I characterise leisure as time spent pleasurably, when I'm not bored and not doing paid work. I may be working in the sense that I am active physically and/or mentally but what I am doing, I am doing because I want to and at the speed I want. I am not fulfilling obligations to others. I might be doing things that please others, but service to them is not my primary motive. If I choose to mend my clothes, then that is a leisure activity. If I don't want to do it, the garments are either thrown away or I pay someone else to do the repairs. If I'm forced to repair them because I'm broke and can't afford new ones, then repairing them is not a leisure activity.

Many of the studies I have read of women's attitude to paid work have been of women doing work that, although they may get a sense of satisfaction out of it, there is little or no indication whether or not they enjoy the work itself. Often they find the company and the environment congenial and a source of support (see, for example, classics like *Women's Leisure, What Leisure?* (Green et al. 1990) and *Brothers* (Cockburn 1983)). In the case of these new IT studies it is clear that the work itself does bring a great deal of pleasure and that this enjoyment has become an important part of the job. Here the question of the balance between work and leisure seems to be being recast yet again. If we take what these women say at face value, 'leisure' as I have characterised it above doesn't seem to figure greatly in their lives.

The concept of 'work/life balance' in the context of these surveys is about balancing paid work on the one hand and domestic and additional work on the other; it seems that leisure time is secondary to the latter two types of work. There is just no time for leisure when obligations to one's family demand, and are given, priority. This difficulty of finding enough time to, say, spend with the children is made even greater when one brings in the further requirement that they be given 'quality time'. I am using the phrase 'quality time' with its usual meaning of time that fits with the rhythm of the children's lives which may or may not conflict with the rhythm of the parents' 'paid work' time.

As an aside, it is worth noting that in the UK, and probably elsewhere, 'resigning one's job to spend more time with the family' has become a common reason for leaving a job when the real reason is less than flattering. 'Being with the family' is nowadays a moral reason for leaving a job and hence can be used a face-saver. Although it appears to be an endorsement of the importance of the family, to my mind there is often an undercurrent of cynical disrespect for the values apparently being invoked – a message that is clear to those who know the real truth. In reality the value incorporated in this high-sounding rhetoric is being subverted.

But let us get back to the balance in women's lives. It is apparent that enough pleasure and enjoyment is derived from this IT work to satisfy the presumed need for leisure activities. Sufficient social interaction with others is derived from the work environment and it is obligations to the family and community that are threatened, not leisure.

"The personal relationships that grow out of the frenetic environment are great. Work is, for better or for worse, a replacement for neighborhood communities these days." (Gewirtz & Lindsey 2015, p. 6)

8.5 Winning Some Time

So, according to the Gewirtz & Lindsey report, many women in the hi-tech industry are very dissatisfied with the long hours they have to work in order to keep up. They need more time for a personal mix of domestic and other obligations as well as for leisure. On the grounds that "We know that women's experience often reflects what is occurring in the larger environment", these authors speculate that men too are beginning to feel this dissatisfaction (p. 4), but perhaps they do not feel it so keenly because it is the women who still feel that they bear the ultimate responsibility. For this reason, these women are rather like the canary taken down coal mines to warn of the presence of methane gas and thus high-risk conditions (Computerworld 2001). If women were to refuse more and more to accept the whole of this responsibility, men would grow even more dissatisfied with the long hours and at that point something effective could be done about the problem. All organisations (commercial and others) who ignore the early warning signs run the risk that the "compelling addiction to 'faster, smarter, newer'" which has kept organisations competitive may become a time-bomb which will damage them. Women would have the force of the firms' own self-interest behind them if these women were to refuse to accept the ultimate responsibility, thus putting more pressure on men to demand change too.

Women's refusal to accept the full responsibility for domestic work is therefore a key factor.

In a lecture Virginia Woolf gave on her own professional experiences in 1931 she wrote about a phantom she called the Angel in the House. This was a woman who often tried to stand between Woolf and her writing. The Angel was one aspect of the perfect woman, wife and mother, sacrificing herself to her family who whispered in Woolf's ear as she wrote a review of a novel by famous man:

> 'My dear you are a young woman. You are writing about a book that has been written by a man. Be sympathetic; be tender; flatter; deceive; use all the arts and wiles of our sex. Never let anybody guess that you have a mind of your own. Above all be pure.' And she made as if to guide my pen. I now record the one act for which I take some credit to myself, though the credit rightly belongs to some excellent ancestors of mine who left me a certain sum of money – shall we say five hundred pounds a year – so that it was not necessary for me to depend solely on charm for my living. I turned upon her and

caught her by the throat. I did my best to kill her . . . Thus whenever I felt the shadow of her wing or the radiance of her halo upon my page, I took up the inkpot and flung it at her. She died hard. (Woolf 1993, Appendix II)

Our contemporary Angel in the House is by no means dead; she whispers a parallel but different message these days. She whispers to each of us "You are, of course, free to earn a living and in a manner you find satisfying; you may excel in business, commerce, IT or the law; but don't ever forget that those dependents for whom you care, children, aged relatives, are ultimately your dependents and nobody else's. Your family needs you and you are the one who has to hold it together." We have by no means killed the phantom and it's going to take a lot of courage to finish her off and we shall be called all sorts of names for doing so.

Virginia Woolf claimed that writing was an easy profession to enter because ink and paper were cheap; so she could afford to use her inkpot to kill the Angel. Laptops are not so replaceable and not so easy to fling; but that Angel must die. We must each and every one of us find the courage to let go those domestic responsibilities that eat up so much of our lives and we must ensure that others take up their part of these obligations to ensure that we can all live more complete lives. And we must persuade the industry as a whole and each and every employer to recognise that this constant search for 'faster, smarter, newer' is in fact damaging women's lives.

CHAPTER 9

JUST HOW MUCH HAS CHANGED?

When it comes to silencing women, Western culture
has had thousands of years of practice.
(Beard 2017, p. xi)

9.1 History of Women in STEM

9.1.1 The Remembered Few: C17 to C19

LONDA SCHIEBINGER IN HER book *The Mind has no Sex?* (Schiebinger 1991) focuses on the role of women in the origins of modern science. While the disciplines covered in this book did not figure in those early days, Schiebinger casts light for us on how these histories have influenced science today. Amongst the numerous women Schiebinger has researched two stand out – both German astronomers: Maria Kirch (or Winkelmann) and Caroline Herschel. There are two main reasons for highlighting these. The first is their achievements. The second is the tradition and the circumstances in which they, and the many others whom Schiebinger mentions, worked. And for Maria Winkelmann particularly the indignities she suffered which continue to this day.

First let us examine the then prevalent traditions. In Germany in the late sixteenth and early seventeenth century astronomy was considered a guild or a craft trade in which the work was carried on in family observatories. Women as wives, sisters and daughters were therefore easily engaged in this while they simultaneously carried out household duties. They learnt from parents, husbands, neighbours and siblings and later became apprentices or assistants to brothers and husbands who were their masters. There they engaged fully in the astronomical work of performing observations, making calculations, keeping records and gaining knowledge of and experience with the technology.

Maria Margaretha Kirch née Winkelmann (1670–1720) *German astronomer*

Maria had an interest in astronomy from early in life and was trained by a local self-taught astronomer. She married Gottfried Kirch, a leading German astronomer some thirty years her senior, and worked closely with him conducting and recording astronomical observations and producing calendars. These calendars predicted astronomical events and became a valuable source of income for the newly formed Berlin Academy of Sciences (1700). In 1702 she discovered a hitherto unknown comet (which was accorded her husband's name, although he did in 1710 acknowledge her role in this discovery). She produced astrological pamphlets and earned a favourable reputation for an astronomical pamphlet which predicted the arrival of a new comet. Leibniz, who respected and supported Winkelmann, wrote of her in a letter of introduction:

> There is [in Berlin] a most learned woman who could pass as a rarity. Her achievement is not in literature or rhetoric but in the most profound doctrines of astronomy . . .(Schiebinger 1991, p. 87)

However, when her husband Gottfried died in 1710 things changed. She was not even considered for the post of astronomer to replace Gottfried in spite of her reputation, experience and productivity. She applied to become an assistant astronomer at the Academy; a submission which was generally not favourably viewed. The Academy's secretary wrote to Leibniz:

> That she be kept on in an official capacity to work on the calendar or to continue with observations simply will not do. Already during her husband's lifetime, the society was burdened with ridicule because its calendar was prepared by a woman. Mouths would gape even wider. (Schiebinger 1991, p. 92)

She found some work, but eventually could no longer work at the Berlin Academy and found employment (unpaid) in a private laboratory as a 'master' astronomer making observations and publishing reports.

Her son, Christfried, was later appointed observer for the Academy and the family again worked in Berlin with Maria as his assistant. In 1717 she was reprimanded for talking too much to visitors to the observatory and it was suggested she should be seen as little as possible at the observatory, especially on public occasions. (This is precisely the point Mary Beard makes in her lecture 'The Public Voice of Women' (Beard 2017)). In short, if you don't do as we say: stop speaking and keep out of the limelight or you will be required to relinquish your post. It was reported "Frau Kirch meddles too much." (Schiebinger 1991, p. 97) She was eventually forced by the Academy to leave the observatory and the house that went with the work, although they hoped she might find a house nearby so she could continue to feed her son who was still in the employ of the observatory. This mirrors situations so often seen. Maria was by the standards of her time a 'trouble maker'. She wanted recognition and, as a widow, the wherewithal to look after her family. Ridicule, attempts to silence her, little recognition of her achievements, none of these persuaded her to go until she was forced out of her academic work. Yet the academy still wanted her to provide domestic support for her son. This was not unusual: "[guild] wives were of such import to production that every guild master was required by law to have one" (Schiebinger 1991, p. 82). So, to cap it all, they totally disregarded her scientific achievements and yet still wanted her to continue with the domestic work.

Maria retired from view and died in 1720 aged 50. The craft trade which had facilitated her career and the careers of others was disappearing as the public scientific institutions were leading the way in employment and prestige. As a result of these changes women who previously by virtue of family and other connections found scope for their talents, if with little or no reward, were beginning lose even these opportunities. Without more education, access to the Universities was, as it always had been, difficult. What is so interesting about the life of Maria Kirch that Schiebinger has unearthed and reported, is the detail – the attempts to belittle her and deny her justice.

Caroline Herschel (1750–1848)
German astronomer

During the eighteenth century some continued to work within this tradition. Caroline Herschel was another German astronomer far better known nowadays than Winkelmann although hers is a slightly different tale. She was not encouraged much in her early life. She was raised in Hamburg, moving later to Bath and London as assistant in various capacities to her brother William. William developed a keen interest in astronomy in which Caroline too started to take an interest. She supported him and acquired the skills necessary for an astronomer including astronomical observations, recording and reducing/compressing astronomical data and organising her brother's work.

She made significant contributions to the discipline; her output was impressive and she was able to publish some of her findings in scientific journals. She received commendation from the Royal Society and won the attention of European astronomers. She was rewarded with a pension of £50 from King George III.

Caroline was the first woman to be awarded a Gold Medal of the Royal Astronomical Society in 1828. She was also named an Honorary Member of the Royal Astronomical Society in 1835 together with the mathematician Mary Somerville as the first women members of the Society.

It is not easy to speculate what either of these two German astronomers would have achieved with better opportunities. Their circumstances and temperaments were different: Maria Kirch had dependent daughters; Caroline Herschel had none. While Maria was forced out, Caroline had always been dutiful, generally doing what was required of her; she at one time described herself as a "well trained puppy dog" (Schiebinger 1991, p. 262), eventually returning to Hamburg and dying there at the age of 97.

Here was a field in which circumstances allowed women to contribute, if only under the patronage of men. For whatever reasons, those in power chose not to continue to embrace the practical crafts in this form and thus excluded the practices along with their women practitioners.

Mary Somerville (1780–1872)
Scottish mathematician and astronomer

Mary Somerville has long been well recognised with multiple honours and awards and an Oxford College has been named after her. In her early life she had little encouragement to obtain a wide education. However, gradually, with the help of family acquaintances she started to educate herself widely in various fields, not least in mathematics and astronomy. Her first husband did not have faith in a woman's capacity to pursue academic and scientific study and so offered her scant encouragement in her scholarly interests. Following his death she remarried and her new husband provided her with every support; they lived and circulated in London mixing with the most eminent scientists of the time, in which society Mary was deeply respected.

Mary Somerville was especially passionate about the links between astronomy and mathematics. Her translation and expansion of Pierre Laplace's *Mécanique Céleste* published as *The Mechanism of the Heavens* in 1831 won her much acclaim.

Her book On the Connexion of the Physical Sciences provided both clear and profound descriptions of such varied matters as the trajectories and anticipated arrival of comets and the commonalities of heat, light and sound. In an anonymous review of this book William Whewell coined the word 'scientist' to describe her partly because of the interdisciplinarity of her subject matter (Anon 1834).[17] There were other works too: *Physical Geography* (1848), which was commonly used as a text until the early 20th century, and *Molecular and Microscopic Science* (1869). She was, in short, a polymath.

Her daughter compiled her memoirs published after her death (Somerville 2016). In the second manuscript of her memoirs E.C. Patterson quotes her as writing the following revealing passage.

> In the climax of my great success, the approbation of some of the first scientific men of the age and of the public in general I was highly gratified, but much less elated than might have been expected, for although I had recorded in a clear point of view some of the most refined and difficult analytical processes and astronomical discoveries, I was conscious that I had never made a discovery myself, that I had no originality. I have perseverance and intelligence but no genius, that spark from heaven is not granted to the sex, we are of the earth, earthy, whether high powers may be alotted [sic] to us in another state of existence God knows, original genius in science is hopeless in this. (Patterson 2012, p. 89)

As Kathryn Neeley suggests this passage reflects Somerville's conflict about wanting women to excel in intellectual pursuits on the one hand and an internal debate as to what women's role really was. (Neeley 2001, p. 188) The long-term effects of such doubts on later generations, even if privately held, are difficult to judge

Ada Lovelace (1815–1852)
English mathematician

It seems doubtful that Ada Lovelace would have shown quite as much humility in her short life as Mary did. Ada's history and accomplishments are well documented (e.g. (Toole 1998; Woolley 1999)). She was the daughter of Lord Byron and Isabella Milbanke who separated shortly after her birth. She was brought up by her mother who ensured that she had a sound education particularly in mathematics (see Section 5.2). She took to mathematics and retained an interest in this throughout her adult life. Her social position meant that like Somerville she mixed with eminent scientists and it was Somerville who introduced her to Charles Babbage. She worked closely with Babbage and is mainly renowned for her work on his Analytical Engine. She recognised that this machine could do more than purely calculate and perceptively noted that if it could manipulate numbers it could manipulate other symbols more generally like letters or musical notes. Her reputation as the first computer programmer is challenged by some who suggest that Babbage had written the programs some years earlier, that there is no evidence that she wrote programs for Babbage's machines nor did she have the skills to write them (Bromley 1990). However nobody has challenged her foresight on what computers could encompass.

She was involved in a few scandals, fairly low-level by modern standards, dying at the young age of 37 of uterine cancer. One lasting memorial to her is the naming of a programming language Ada: a high level, structured language designed for the Department of Defense in the US between 1977 and 1983.

Sofia Kovalevskaia (1850–1891)
Russian mathematician

Sofia Kovalevskaia was a distinguished mathematician whose impressive achievements were realised within a seemingly contradictory world in the latter half of the nineteenth century. Born into a reasonably affluent Russian household she mixed with a tolerant and progressive intelligentsia. The 1860s in Russia saw the early days of the nihilism movement whose adherents advocated social reform, were in favour of equality between the sexes and believed that women had a duty and a right to educate themselves. At the same time there was a renewed interest in science and women were being encouraged to study natural science and medicine. As a young woman growing up in Russia, Sofia had been provided with a sound early education, was tutored in mathematics and obtained access to radical literature. However entry into Russian universities was not possible so many entered into 'fictitious marriages' [18] to enable them to move abroad for study. Sofia did just this and subsequently went to Heidelberg. Here she had to approach Heidelberg professors to be allowed to attend lectures in mathematics and physics. She acquitted herself well so, when she later moved to Berlin, she went with strong recommendations from two Heidelberg professors. In Berlin she worked closely with and was taught privately by the renowned mathematician Weierstrass. Under his guidance and with his support she completed one of her most famous proofs on partial differential equations. This formed part of her submission for a doctorate in mathematics at the University of Göttingen for which she was awarded *summa cum laude*, the first woman anywhere to hold this degree. Recall that we saw in Section 5.4 how PJ Möbius writing in 1907 expressed, for the period, some unsurprising views on Kovalevskaia - and others.

Later, in 1883, Kovalevskaia moved to Stockholm University and eventually became the only woman in Europe to have a university level teaching post. In the face of prejudice and antagonism from reactionaries, she remained consistently radical about social issues.

She subsequently became a salaried professor and in 1889, just two years before her early death from pneumonia at the age of 41, was appointed to a full and lifetime professorship.

Her work in mechanics and mathematical physics continued throughout the last years of her life. The best known piece of work from this period is on the rotation of a solid body about a fixed point, the 'Kovalevskaia top' for which she was awarded the *Prix Bordin* of the French Academy of Sciences, and for this she was widely acclaimed. She paid a heavy price for this; travelling to Paris to receive it she contracted pneumonia which led to her death.

Throughout her life Sofia was an ardent and lively activist not only on behalf of women but was always interested in other radical causes. Ann Hibner Koblitz's biography (Koblitz 1983) draws attention to this and notes how it was not only being a woman in a newly emerging scientific world that caused Kovalevskaia problems, but also her reputation as a radical and, moreover, a Russian radical who had 'escaped' to Europe.

9.1.2 Were there any commonalities between these five scientists?

It is tempting to suggest that these five people were alike in some way. The only really prominent feature they shared, apart from a love of mathematics, is self-motivation and the ability to self-teach. They were, unsurprisingly, of very different temperaments. They all gained a reputation in their time and circulated amongst famous scientists, they all published papers. Only three are recorded as having been paid in their own right and of course none of them had easy access to a university education. Only one was awarded a doctorate and she became a life-time professor. In spite of their pioneering work, they are rarely mentioned nowadays in science courses at any level of education with the exception of Ada Lovelace. Sofia Kovalevskaia is recognised in the academic world through the US-based Association for Women in Mathematics which sponsors the annual Kovalevsky Lectures awarded to anyone in the scientific or engineering community whose work highlights the achievements of women in applied or computational mathematics. (*Association for Women in Mathematics* 2020) There is a Kovalevskaia fund to support women in science in developing countries.

Outside academia they do have some recognition. There are now events bearing the name of Ada Lovelace (*Ada Lovelace Day Online 2020*; *Ada Lovelace Festival* 2020) and a television documentary explaining her work and life (Fry 2015). Recognitions for Mary Somerville have already been mentioned and she now features on the Scottish £10 note (Piper 2017). A lunar crater has been named in her honour. There was a movie made about Sofia Kovalevskaia, called appropriately *A Hill on the Dark Side of the Moon* (in Swedish: Berget På Månens Baksida).

9.2 The Twentieth Century and the Half-remembered

9.2.1 The Women of Bletchley Park in World War II

Modern computing was conceived in the military context of World War II (WWII). Bletchley Park was the central wartime site for the Government Code and Cipher School (GC&CS). The story of Bletchley Park is now fairly well known particularly amongst those who have acquired any knowledge of the history of computing. Code breakers and cryptanalysts employed there penetrated the military communications of the members of the Axis Alliance throughout the war deciphering Enigma and Lorenz codes.[19] Over 10,000 people worked there in utmost secrecy. Of these, 8,000 or approximately 75% were women. Advertisements went out for both men and women to apply. However it was men who overwhelmingly filled the prestigious positions with a few women employed as cryptanalysts. Initially the female recruits came from upper class backgrounds with trusted family connections and were engaged in administrative and clerical work. But as requirements expanded they started to recruit women with maths, engineering, physics and language degrees. So, women became employed in many crucial auxiliary capacities operating cryptographic and communications machinery, translation, traffic analysis. By the end of 1944 more than half the women employed at Bletchley Park were serving in the British Armed Forces. The extraordinary skill of the cryptanalysts who broke the Enigma and Lorenz code and devised the bombe and Colossus[20] and so on has overshadowed the diligent, dull and repetitive work of the huge cohort of women who ensured the whole thing worked, although because of strict security they had little knowledge of what they were contributing to and what was going on around them. (*Women in Bletchley Park* 2018)

The relevant skills at cryptography and so on of these dominant men were crucial and they have achieved deserved status but the gender division of work and strict secrecy surrounding the site meant that the work of the women was hidden. They had signed the Official Secrets Act and many were loath to talk about it even when free to do so from 1975. Some even did not speak of their work until the 1990's, if at all. Modern Bletchley Park staff tell how a couple were visiting one day when the husband told his wife: "You know, I used to work here." Her eyes widened, as she also confessed to have worked there too, but in a different hut. They had been married to each other for over 30 years!

The organisation supporting so many employees at Bletchley Park and surrounding sites was extraordinary. Some aspects of communication between departments were primitive (motor bikes to convey messages for example) and yet secrecy was maintained. The sense of loyalty to the Allied cause and a traditional respect for 'King and Country' meant that, unsurprisingly, everybody obeyed the rules and carried them to extraordinary lengths until well after the end of the war. Alan Turing and other men became household names certainly in the UK, but none of the women's did until quite recently. When interviewed they appeared shy about talking about their contribution, all of which adds another layer to the masking of their work.

Dillwyn "Dilly" Knox, one well known cryptographer, asked to have only women on his team and the women accepted this policy as unexceptional. Knox was respectful towards them and fully recognised their skills, giving two of them full recognition for a significant break of the German Intelligence Abwehr code. But this group of female specialists were and still are known as 'Dilly's Fillies' or 'Dilly's Girls'. (Ridley 2015)

Much of this has become a template for the roles of men and women in the subsequent burgeoning of computing. Women were invisibly doing most of the work including tasks that it had been felt they might not be able to. (*Women in Bletchley Park* 2018) While men were seen to design and build the hardware, women operated it; the men were acclaimed and the women forgotten.

Before moving on to other stories about the work of women in wartime and in the US, there's another point which needs highlighting from a gender perspective – it concerns a form of address in these 'academic scientific' environments. The advertisements for work at Bletchley Park stated they were looking for 'men of the professor type' and in the first instance recruitment was from Cambridge and Oxford subsequently employing others and particularly women as demand grew. I raise this point in the light of Mary Beard's question about positions of power. What do we imagine when we hear the title 'professor'? As Beard, herself a professor, observes

> If we close our eyes and try to conjure up the image of . . . a professor, what most of us see is not a woman. And it is just as true even if you are a woman professor: . . . it is still hard for me to imagine me, or someone like me, in my role. (Beard 2017, pp. 53–54)

This title of 'professor' has been associated with men for centuries, but by the 1940s it had gone a bit further, establishing the title as implying a powerful position which the addressed person did not, necessarily, have.

Often the men at Bletchley Park were addressed as 'Prof' as was

Alan Turing and referred to as 'the Prof' even though he never held the title of Professor (even if he should have eventually). Joan Clarke who worked with him and was quite close to him said he expressed some discomfort with that form of address (Hodges 1992, p. 208). Other senior men at Bletchley Park were addressed and referred to in the same way. It had become a norm and still is in university science departments although it is largely men who use this form of address; it is a form of respect. I have never heard a female professor addressed in this way, nor do I hear women use it to or of male professors. Meanings change – that's inevitable – but this change is more refined than that, it seems to reinforce the exclusion of women. It may be that this is a phenomenon that only occurs in science departments in the UK, but it has been there for decades, to my certain knowledge, and has always felt as if it is reinforcing the idea of a male science club with a respected male boss.

Returning now to the thread that while men were seen to design and build the hardware, women operated it; the men were acclaimed and the women forgotten, the ENIAC 'girls' provide another classical example. The ENIAC - heralded as the first programmable digital computer – was built and launched in the US at the end of and following WWII. It was developed to calculate trajectories for armaments. It has been said that "Men were interested in building the hardware . . . Doing the circuits, figuring out the machinery." "but the grueling and tedious task of creating programs for it was considered 'women's work,' akin to clerical labor." (Timeline 2017) But in reality it wasn't quite like that. They did programming, which although it had, broadly speaking, the same relationship to hardware as software does today, it required a more intimate knowledge of the machines and processes. They remained unrecognised for their highly technical and successful work for over 50 years; they were not invited to the celebratory meal following its first demonstration nor even, according to a documentary maker, to the 50th anniversary party (ENIAC Programmers Project Documentary Team 2010). However, more recently they have begun to receive more recognition e.g. Alyson Sheppard (Sheppard 2013). There is archival evidence mentioned in a video hosted by the Computer History Museum in California and authored by Thomas Haigh (Haigh 2017) and in a book (Haigh et al. 2018) in which he demonstrates that it is very likely that women were being paid for doing the same type of work as men when the machine was under construction. So, although they appear to have been involved in building the machine and were deeply involved in the programming, it is still the senior men John W Mauchly and J Presper Eckert who get the glory and honour for this (Freiberger & Swaine 2008).

Although much of these women's work couldn't be directly compared with writing modern software or programming it had almost the same relationship to the hardware. Why a 'template'? For example, men started the computer revolution (for that's what these developments ultimately if not obviously directly became), it was made to appear that women assisted, got involved with it and did what was expected of them and in the tradition that prevailed. Post WWII many younger women became programmers, but gradually their numbers dwindled and the new generations of computers are run by and for men.

So the women of Bletchley Park are 'half-remembered' in that they were almost unheard of until the mid-1970s; likewise the ENIAC girls who are only now really appearing in the limelight and gaining some prominence. Their individual names are not as well-known as Alan Turing and "Dilly" Knox. The names of the ENIAC women are (or perhaps we could now say were) better known. The efforts of these women are still not brought to the attention of students during their Computer Science degree courses. Some might ask 'How can we include them, where would such information fit into the curriculum?' The difficulty in finding answers to those questions is in itself revealing. Their names and stories are published and can be read. Their power and influence can come from their reputation as a body. Something I shall return to.

9.2.2 And After WWII

Advances in space science provided another massive change that occurred in the decades following WWII. So I now turn attention to the role of a particular group of women contributing to wartime efforts in aeronautics and subsequently their contributions to space travel – black women. While the space industry celebrated men in orbit and landing on the moon, it failed to tell the stories of the women involved in their success and in particular the accounts of African American women. 'Victory through air power!' was one slogan encouraging efforts to develop and refine aircraft production in the US from 1941 onwards. People with all types of relevant skills were needed to prosecute this including mathematicians, so eventually they were conscripting large numbers of, initially, white women graduates to work at Langley.

They were employed as mathematicians or 'computers', as they were then called, working for NASA and its predecessor NACA (National Advisory Committee for Aeronautics) at the Langley Research Centre, Virginia. The defence industry was desegregated by Executive Order in June 1941, thus opening the way for African Americans to work in aeronautics.

From 1943 black women who had graduated in science and mathematics from local segregated colleges began to respond to advertisements to work as mathematicians and computers. Many had gone into teaching following graduation which often meant they were more experienced than their white counterparts.

The book *Hidden Figures* by Margot Lee Shetterly (Shetterly 2017) tells the stories of three of these women, coming from broadly similar background and locality, who met at Langley but eventually pursued different paths. Shetterly's account of the working lives of these three, embedded as it is in extensive background material about Langley and of segregated lives, makes for compulsive reading. Shetterly emphasizes that there are more, possibly many more, untold stories like these.

For those of us who have never lived in a segregated world,

the repeated occurrence of the word 'colored' is a shock and serves to emphasise just what these women had to deal with in addition to what we white women have had to tolerate. Segregation on the buses bringing people to and from work, segregation in housing, segregation in the cafeteria where a notice designated special tables for 'COLORED COMPUTERS', segregated drinking fountains, different coffee pots, segregated wash-rooms signified by 'COLORED LADIES ROOM' (demeaningly placed so that it was considerably further for those who had to use them and moreover requiring them to walk outside in all weathers) and, possibly most significantly, separate rooms to work in.

The first of our three women to arrive at Langley was Dorothy Vaughan (1910 – 2008) (*Dorothy Vaughan* 2018) who in 1943 aged 32 was appointed to a job at Langley as a mathematician, at double her current pay as a teacher; a job she, as a keen mathematician, had no hesitation in taking. She worked at Langley, initially in a room of women operating calculators known as the West Area Computer Section to process the data produced by engineers testing the aerodynamics of new designs. She rose to be supervisor of the section until it was disbanded. As mechanical computers began to take over the role of the human computers Vaughan taught herself Fortran and moved into a new building housing an IBM machine where she was instrumental in encouraging women to join her in this transition. Although in fact at this point of inflection, as computing moved from human computers run by an all-female cohort to mechanical or electronic devices, men started to move in and take control.

The second 'computer' was Katherine Goble Johnson (1918 – 2020) (*Katherine Johnson* 2020) who, having showed exceptional mathematical ability from a very early age, arrived at West Area Computer Section at Langley in 1953. Later reassigned to Spacecraft Controls Branch she made significant contributions to the calculations for space fight; calculating in 1961 the trajectory for the first American in space and the launch window for the Mercury mission the same year, and producing other navigation charts for use in the event of electronic failure. By 1962 and John Glenn's space orbit, mechanical computers were calculating trajectories not human computers, but John Glenn refused to fly unless Johnson checked the figures – he asked for her specifically. A white male cosmonaut in a still segregated country insisting on being reassured by the calculations of an African American woman that it was safe for him to fly! Her work continued into plans for lunar landings, space shuttle programs and plans for a mission to Mars.

Katherine Johnson received numerous accolades during her lifetime including the Presidential Medal of Freedom and a research building at Langley named after her.

The third of these women was Mary Jackson (1921 – 2005) (*Mary Jackson* 2018). She joined West Area Computer Section at Langley in 1951 working under Dorothy Vaughan's supervision. Her yearning was for engineering, and in 1953 she accepted an offer to work for an engineer in the Supersonic Pressure Tunnel studying forces generated by winds over twice the speed of sound. She succeeded in obtaining entry to an all-white college to obtain the qualifications necessary to enable her to qualify as an aerospace engineer, to which role she was promoted in 1958 – NASA's first black female engineer. From then on she worked in various NASA engineering divisions analysing data from wind tunnel and real air flight experiments. In 1979, having achieved the most senior engineering title within the engineering department, she turned her attention to equal opportunities and encouraging changes for women and minorities before retiring from NASA in 1985.

Like so many others, each of these women had children and had to make arrangements for their care. This responsibility on top of demeaning language used to address them and segregated spaces are just some examples of a gendered situation which so many women are still fighting. But for these women their race made their situations far more challenging.

These stories highlight how intersectional politics impact employment and research programmes. Racism and sexism are both still rife in our society and, while segregation of races or genders is no longer legal, they remain lodged in individual and institutional thinking and in attitudes to technology and computer development. Obviously, towards the end of the twentieth century there were other massive changes in science and technology bringing equally massive increases in speed of communication and so on. It would therefore be a reasonable expectation that women of all races and ethnicities would be far more advanced in their participation and success in modern sciences and technologies or STEM subjects (Science, Technology, Engineering and Mathematics – which also of course encompass computing). But as we have already seen there has been astonishingly little improvement.

And this is in spite of much effort since the early 1990s and before with many, mainly women, working to increase the female participation rate. What role did women who had influence and power have to play in all this? Plenty of prominent women scientists can be named and in the case of computing there have been for example: Grace Hopper, Anita Borg, Stephanie Shirley and Wendy Hall, to highlight only a few. What difference have they and all the others truly made as role models and exemplars?

Women who achieve success in these areas have indeed reached a pinnacle; their very scarcity helps to make them prominent. Although many have worked hard to attract more women and have spoken out on behalf of women, how much effect have they had in increasing numbers and in raising the profile of those already working in the industry? The answers to those questions are of course unknown; they may have had some influence but given technological and other social changes one would expect it would have been much greater.

What stands out now is how, during the late 1990s when some of us made considerable efforts in this area, how alone we were, just women working at it. Men didn't get involved for many reasons. For one they weren't attuned to exactly what was happening or what was lacking; few women was the norm and they, by virtue of their conditioning and hegemony, knew well how to keep them in their place with the assistance of their peers. Obviously, competition has always been important amongst men and reducing the extent and threat of this helps them succeed in retaining their personal reputation. Once this state of affairs is accepted by the majority no-one has to question why it is happening; it's other people's problem. The men won't accrue kudos if they are seen to try to increase the presence of women; not least because they would be spending time doing that rather than the more significant work which is advancing their very discipline. But surely the near absence of women is more important? Who are these practitioners to say that what they do is more important? The answer lies partly in accepted practices throughout academia. But in computing as in other STEM subjects, practitioners have been difficult to challenge because they always had the kudos. Science from the Greeks onwards was the prerogative of men and this dominance has remained unassailable.

It is perhaps timely here to quote again from John Stuart Mill's book *The Subjection of Women* published in 1869 (a quotation I used as an epigraph in 1996).

> Think what it is to a boy, to grow up to manhood in the belief that without any merit or exertion of his own, though he may be the most frivolous and empty or the most ignorant and stolid of mankind, by the mere fact of being born a male he is by right the superior of all and every one of an entire half of the human race: including probably some whose real superiority to himself he has daily or hourly occasion to feel . . . (Mill 1869, p. 148–149)[21]

How much has changed in 150 years? In many fields there has been movement: politics, journalism, the law, and perhaps medicine and biology and their related industries, which now tend to be seen more as women's subjects. But in the STEM industries, not a lot, I suggest – so far.

Here are a couple of personal examples to illustrate what can happen and the personal aspect is important because my internal reactions illustrate what so often happens. My book *Women and Computers* published in 1996 attracted good reviews. I cite one review from the Times Higher Educational Supplement: "This book should be compulsory reading for those connected with the ever-widening computer industry, all of whom should be interested in the social issues raised" (Whitehouse 1997, p. 30). To my knowledge it was scarcely discussed within my department except when I raised it. A few months after its publication I asked a male colleague at a departmental party if he had any views on it and he simply asked "Hasn't it been remaindered yet?" When asked if he had read it he unsurprisingly replied "No". It is worth noting here that ridicule such as this is now being classified as a form of gender harassment. And a year or so later a senior member of my department spotted a copy of this book on the desk of a female Computing Assistant and asked her rather distastefully "What are you reading that for?"

And another, later, incident. I succeeded in getting the Dean of the Science Faculty to allow me to speak at a faculty meeting on what can be done about the shortage of women in science. At the end there were almost no questions except one memorable one: "Why do we need to bother about this?" Or words to that effect. I had been aware that the questioner had apparently been concentrating on documents in front of him whilst I was speaking.

These incidents which I still recall forcefully after almost two decades illustrate that many of the potential audiences for my book and the short talk were just not interested, not prepared to address the subject and that this indifference was acceptable to them and their colleagues. These incidents to me then and now are horrifying and at the time they silenced me. How is it people adopted such an immoral stance and why was I almost silenced?

9.3 The Twenty-First Century

Mary Somerville's concern about women's role continues in pockets to this day and occasionally it can be even more pronounced.

It turns out that just like so many other organisations: broadcasting, entertainment, the Churches, Government (inside and outside parliament) and aid agencies, the tech industry has been forcefully and effectively helping to continue the subordination of women.

Emily Chang, an American journalist, in her recent book *Brotopia: Breaking up the Boys' Club of Silicon Valley* (Chang 2018) gives numerous examples of what has been happening to women in Silicon Valley since the collapse of the dot-com bubble and the growth of venture capital enterprises. Her analysis starts with the rise and adulation of the 'nerd' or 'anorak' mentality in the 1990s (although it had appeared in many western countries up to two decades before that). Aptitude tests for identifying programmers not only tested for those who liked puzzles, had spatial skills and so on but for those interested in things rather than people. This combined with the awe in which these 'experts' were held for what they appeared to be achieving and allowed them to become powerful stereotypes in the industry for those whom CEOs and everybody else were keen to employ. But it's highly likely that it started long before that and its origins can be traced back to what was happening at Bletchley Park during WWII. My own experience of employment in the UK confirms what is often reported - that women programmers were disappearing in the late 1960s and the nerds were firmly established in power by the early 1970s.

To return to what was happening in Silicon Valley. In spite of the dot-com crash these same people and the values they espoused were waiting and ready to restart and engage in making money and creating the ethos that now exists in Silicon Valley.

Chang's impressive record of her 200 interviews and the wide range of problems women told her makes compulsive reading for those of us who have been through even a fraction of what she describes her contacts had to endure. It's the usual list of incidents and occurrences that impact the personal life and the career: the micro-inequities, or 'Little Things' as one of Chang's interviewees calls them, and the big things - overt sexual approaches sometimes

24/7, parties with too much alcohol and sex, being expected to work unsocial hours, and so on. Some brave women take on their detractors and attackers, the employers who deny them their rights. Some manage to stay, others get pushed out.

One who took them on was Ellen Pao who sued her employer, a venture capital firm, alleging sexual bias against women. She lost but her case provided the inspiration for a group of women to collect data and stories of women's experiences in the tech industry. Here are just a few statistics from their report *Elephant in the Valley*

- 47% of women have been asked to do lower-level tasks, such as taking notes and ordering food, which men are not asked to do.
- 66% of women have felt left out of important networking events because of their gender.
- 75% of women were asked about their family lives, marital status and children in interviews.

and so on (*Elephant in the Valley* 2017)

Chang reports in detail how men in the tech business, and particularly where she was researching in Silicon Valley, employ in their own image. She also reports how there are some working hard to push back at this phenomenon. Many note it when asked but clearly do not want to do anything about it; nor are they likely to. It's not just that they simply employ men, they employ men who are literally in their own image (or very near it): chase money, chase women, chase a go-getting life style and one where working a 90 hour week at one's family's expense is to be encouraged. [22]

It is sometimes said that extreme anti-feminist views, as expressed for example by Peter Thiel (a conservative libertarian, co-founder of PayPal and well respected in some circles in Silicon Valley), aren't expressed any more. He wrote in a blog on the libertarian journal *Cato Unbound* in April 2009:

> Since 1920, the vast increase in welfare beneficiaries and the extension of the franchise to women – two constituencies that are notoriously tough for libertarians – have rendered the notion of "capitalist democracy" into an oxymoron. (Thiel 2009)

A computer engineer employed by Google provoked an international outcry when he published a document saying biological gender differences make women less effective programmers and that Google should desist from its work in promoting diversity (Damore 2017). There is much one could quote from this document for present purposes but the following footnote will suffice: "For heterosexual romantic relationships, men are more strongly judged by status and women by beauty. Again, this has biological origins and is culturally universal." The employee, James Damore, was fired following the outcry. While many condemned the Damore's note, the author's views had some support from, for example, a Google employee posting on an anonymous message board:

> Can we go back to the time when Silicon Valley [was] about nerds and geeks, that's why I applied [to] Google and came to the US. I mean this industry used to be a safe place for people like us . . . (Booth & Hern 2017)

9.4 Power

The why and how of the minute improvements which have occurred in women's position in STEM subjects are difficult to unravel. We've looked at some of the why: men's millennia long conviction that they know best as well as the complex interactions amongst men. This traditional belief in male superiority becomes normalised and accepted by society and enables men to continue to move into positions of power. Then there is also the other half of this, women's complicity and their reluctance *as a body* to critique this state of affairs to put themselves forward and to engage wholeheartedly and productively in the competitive technological world. Making such a criticism of the female body politic was an unspoken taboo – unsisterly. But it has been, and it still remains, the case that it is the mass of the female politic which has done so much to hinder progress.

Following the flood of accusations from October 2017 of sexual misconduct in many spheres, one thing has emerged: women united in their condemnation and the concentration of coverage has been such that "it has swept aside the usual divisions between those nominally on the same side" (Brockes 2017). Such unity is effective, refreshing and rare and has resulted in high powered resignations. This shows what unity amongst women can achieve, if only in the short term. So how are we to shift power?

9.4.1 Mary Beard on Power

The outlook for change through a conventional understanding of what can be achieved through action, education, focussed events and so on appears bleak – particularly in these fields where male domination is so powerfully entrenched. Beard suggests that we should start thinking about power differently. She writes

> . . . this is still treating power as something elite, coupled to public prestige. . . It is also treating power very narrowly, as an object of possession that only the few – mostly men – can own or wield . . . On those terms, women as gender – not as some individuals – are by definition excluded from it. You cannot easily fit women into a structure that is already coded as male; you have to change the structure. That means thinking about power differently. It means decoupling it from public prestige. It means, above

all, thinking about power as an attribute or even a verb ('to power'), not as a possession. (Beard 2017, pp. 86–87)

Beard suggests we are a long way off subverting foundational sources of power that have existed for so long. Nonetheless we can start thinking about what power is, where it comes from and be more aware of the myriad of ways in which it is perpetuated and, if you like, create our own new forms of power.

It is tempting to think that perhaps something in the form of a grass roots movement might be achieved for women employed within STEM. It could happen maybe amongst students – alongside other grass roots movements for young females and women's organisations in professional bodies and in universities. I have never yet heard of student women in tech challenging the *status quo* outside their own feminist groups; it could be they are quite reasonably fearful of ridicule and ostracism from the male elite amongst staff and students. And women, once they have embarked on a computing career, should start 'powering' themselves by kicking aside all those micro-inequities which get in the way of progress.

It is the very overwhelming number of men that continues to hinder movement, and will continue to do so until and unless everybody takes the issue seriously and embraces the rebalancing of power that will occur. Maybe publicising and analysing the efforts and reactions of all those women at Bletchley Park might start to light the way.

PART V
INTERDISCIPLINARITY AND OTHER APPROACHES

CHAPTER 10

WORKING AT THE BOUNDARIES: OPPORTUNITIES AND PROBLEMS FACING INTERDISCIPLINARITY

This chapter was originally published in 'Grenzgänge Genderforschung in Informatik und Naturwissenschaften', Sigrid Schmitz & Britta Schinzel (Eds.) in 2004. It is reproduced here by kind permission of the publisher: Ulrike Helmer Verlag

10.1 How Disciplines Came to Be

THE WORD 'DISCIPLINE' IS commonly used in two different ways which are at first sight quite distinct. There is discipline in the sense of the enforcement of rules, and the punishment of those who transgress them. On the other hand, there is discipline in the sense of an ordered body of related knowledge. In fact they are from the same root and one doesn't have to delve very far to realise that they have overlapping meanings.

The reader may remember how in *Discipline and Punish* Michel Foucault develops the idea of 'docile bodies' that conform to societal norms through a network of disciplinary institutions: schools, universities, employment, prisons, the military, hospitals (both general and psychiatric). Conformity is achieved by a surveillance that establishes norms and corrects deviances. These docile bodies are put into spaces, which are "at once architectural, functional and hierarchical". (Foucault 1977, p. 148) One observer "dreamt [in or around 1783] of a classroom in which the spatial distribution might provide a whole series of distinctions at once: according to the pupils' progress, worth, character, application, cleanliness and parents' fortune" (p. 147). There were, and still are, other educational procedures which helped to heighten discipline: examinations, exercises, a proliferation of tests. All of these contribute towards a docile body, which Foucault argues was necessary for capitalist production.

The second meaning of the word 'discipline' isn't all that unconnected to the first. This is the sense in which 'discipline' refers to a defined body of knowledge and thought. This certainly covers all the scientific disciplines, which have perhaps to some extent their own epistemology, language, methods and modes of argument. They must also of course share certain features if they are properly to be called 'scientific'. For instance, scientists have to check their assertions and statements by observing the world, perhaps by experimentation. This would mean that certain disciplines often referred to as sciences, such as mathematics and computer science should not properly be called sciences. For example, computer scientists do not observe the world in order to check their assertions any more than mathematicians go round measuring the internal angles of triangles to check whether or not these add up to 180°. A mathematician who keeps checking the sum of the angles has mistaken the nature of the discipline and, by breaking its rules, brought him or herself into disrepute as a result.

The two meanings of the word 'discipline' are not all that dissimilar. They intertwine in that there can be a kind of penalty to be paid (often in terms of reputation) for someone who strays outside the area of their discipline or who commits faults (breaks the rules) within that discipline. To disregard the rules is seen as a challenge to the academic authority by the transgressor. To go through several years of study of a discipline is to be trained, schooled, or to be made to think in prescribed ways. It's not only docile bodies, but what could be dubbed 'docile minds' that Foucault is concerned about. There is, of course, no god-given authority that sanctions the carving up of knowledge into the lumps that we have today. "... knowledges are social constructs and practices bearing specific histories" (Leitch 2000). It seems very likely that the disciplines we have today arose from the dynamics of society and that there is a kind of hidden (social) agenda.

The history of mathematics as a discipline provides an example. With the establishment of the scientific revolutions in the seventeenth and eighteenth centuries there came an increasing need for young men to demonstrate their rationality and mastery of the mind/body divide. (Hacker 1990) Skill in mathematics came to be seen as a proof of this. So mathematics eventually replaced Latin and Theology as a general measure of ability. It taught self-discipline and self-restraint. The rules of arithmetic and geometry "will supply accuracy and intelligence for those who follow them"(p. 42).

If, as Foucault argues, modern methods of production needed docile bodies, it also needed trained but docile minds that could think, but yet not challenge the *status quo*. This seems to have been the solution to the problem of educating so many people without producing discontent and a revolutionary class – a high-risk strategy but one that worked. It is significant that the political economy still has this sort of requirement and the University still stubbornly remains organised in departments which reflect disciplines.

Thus 'discipline' in the sense of enforcement of rules and punishment of transgressors and 'discipline' in the sense of an ordered body of related knowledge begin to fuse together.

10.2 The Emergence of Interdisciplinarities

This dividing up of knowledge into discrete areas necessarily creates boundaries. But these boundaries are always on the move, they are shifting, they sometimes overlap, there are gaps; new areas are created by the overlaps, and these occasionally become disciplines themselves. Each discipline can have boundaries with numerous others and thus there is an infinity of possible boundaries. And, although geographical metaphors abound when people talk of interdisciplinarities, it is impossible to build a map to illustrate this, not least because it needs a complex, multi-dimensional space. Interdisciplinarity is one thing that happens at the borders of these disciplines but, by and large, it occurs at the boundaries of *specialties* within those disciplines – not between the disciplines themselves. One feature of interdisciplinary work that arises in at least two guises is 'objects'. In Section 10.6 I discuss 'objects of discourse' a concept that Foucault uses to explain 'madness', for example, which is part of the discourse and changes with it. Secondly, there are 'objects of study', which initially, at least, are fixed and have a meaning for each participating discipline and provide a focus for research. Just as there is an infinity of interdisciplinarities, so too there are numerous forms that each can take. But far from all of them being cases of mutual picking up of disciplinary specialties, some of the examples I give show that sometimes some of the original disciplines are transformed in some way.

The first example is from earth sciences: plate tectonics. Klein (Klein 1996, p. 58) characterises this as 'a comprehensive theory or hypothesis that explains mountain building, earthquakes, and volcanism.' It involved geologists (stratigraphers, paleoclimatologists, tectonisists), oceanographers, geophysicists (seismologists, paleomagnetists), geochemists (geochronologists, volcanologists), geomorphologists, geobiologists (paleobiologists) who had different ways of explaining the same phenomena. It emerged rapidly and surprisingly over the period 1957-70 and was a unifying hypothesis that enabled them all 'to sing from the same hymn sheet'. As Klein points out, this rapid taking up of the theory raises the question "Was the plate tectonics revolution the result of interdisciplinary co-operation at the margins of the disciplines concerned? Or could it be interpreted as a recognition of the impact of principles, theories and data that were all central elements of the different disciplines?" (p. 59). Whatever the answer to these two questions, the significance of this particular interdisciplinarity is an example of a transformation of part of each of the participating disciplines.

The next example is also one that occurred within the natural sciences. Molecular biology represents the skills of physicists, chemists, geneticists, bacteriologists, zoologists and botanists. Its emergence was triggered by the discovery of the structure of DNA. Prior to this, biology was considered a discipline that described organisms and the one that searched for 'the meaning of life'. The collaboration with mainly physicists meant that it was transformed into a discipline that experimented with genetic material – it was interventionist. (Keller 1993) So physics and new technologies had a powerful influence in establishing and underpinning this new version of biology. This example represents the transformation of particularly one of the participating disciplines.

The particular collaboration between physicists and biologists provides a nice example of borrowing between disciplines. There were various ways in which biology borrowed from physics: "first, by borrowing an agenda which was seen as looking like that of physics; second, by borrowing the language and attitude of physicists . . . Indeed, even the borrowing of purely technical expertise, ostensibly in the name of making biology 'better', was instrumental in reframing biology in making it different." (Keller 1993, p. 57) . However, 'borrowing' is possibly a misleading metaphor – if items are borrowed (the agenda, language etc. of physics), they can never be the property of the borrower – biology in this case; they should hand these things back at some point. Perhaps it is better to say simply the biologists used these features of physics.

The interfaces between mathematical specialties and specialties from other disciplines provide some further examples of interest. First, there is mathematics and computer science. The advent of computers after World War II gave rise to further development of complexity theory and the identification of, for example, intractable and undecidable problems and the design and analysis of algorithms. This was often mathematics done by mathematicians who had moved into computer science. It developed into a specialty within computer science using the language and methods of mathematics. It didn't alter either of the contributing disciplines except insofar as it produced new knowledge for both – and no doubt gave the fledgling discipline of computing a more 'scientific' image. In this case neither discipline was radically altered – both were augmented.

Mathematics is engaged in interdisciplinary work with a whole range of other disciplines. What are now classical statistical methods using notions of mathematical deviance and so on were developed for agricultural experimentation, prediction from archaeological finds, psephological methods for predicting election outcomes and sampling techniques for surveys. So, mathematics interfaces with social sciences providing methods and tools and, to an extent, itself benefits from these contacts. It is worth noting at this point that I take up the link between natural and social sciences again in a later section.

Much of what I have been talking about so far happens spontaneously; this seems to leave an element of chance. Michael Gibbons and his colleagues (Gibbons 1994, pp. 3–7), having looked at the methods of knowledge production, put much of this interdisciplinary work on a formal self-conscious basis where the element of chance is reduced. They divide modes of knowledge production into two types: modes 1 and 2. Mode 1 is traditional in that it is primarily academic, homogeneous and hierarchical and emphasises disciplinary boundaries. Mode 2, on the other hand, is transdisciplinary in that the final solution will be beyond that of any contributing discipline; it is about applications in context, heterogeneous in terms of the skills and experience people bring to it; it is socially accountable and reflexive. This gives rise to hybrid communities "consisting of people who have been socialised in different subsystems, disciplines or working environments" (p. 37) coming together in order to systematically look for opportunities for interdisciplinary research. There is a new attitude of mind and a proactive approach.

This second mode of knowledge production is surely one that now features in gender studies, women's studies, cultural studies, queer studies and so on. In each of these (and I shall illustrate this in more detail later) people from many disciplines work together, with the participating disciplines, hopefully, becoming transdisciplinary in the sense I have just alluded to. The word 'hybridity' for these studies suggests offspring of a union of two or more distinct species.

10.3 'Centres', 'Institutes', 'Studies', and Departments

The general tenor is for universities to be organised on disciplinary lines in a manner that is reflected in departmental structures. Various collaborations, with labels like 'Centre', 'Institute' and 'Studies' in their titles, do emerge in which people come together to study topics of common interest that cannot be defined within one discipline. But, ironically enough, as Klein observes, these centres are never at the centre of the academic institution; they are usually 'Centres for X' and are peripheral to the main academic (Klein 1996, p. 28).

They are sometimes alternatively labelled 'Institutes' suggesting something less than a discipline and, perhaps, having a precarious future, which contrasts with the relative strengths and endurance of the established disciplines. Interestingly there were, in 2000, no departments of cultural studies in the US (Leitch 2000) and judging from a quick search this looks the same in 2004. On the other hand, there are many departments of women's studies in the US.

In the UK there is a well-established Institute for Women's Studies at Lancaster University. I mention this because a list of the contributing departments/disciplines/centres etc. to the work of this institute nicely illustrates the hybridity of what is taught and researched there. It also serves to point out what is missing, which is what will be discussed later. The contributors are: Applied Social Science, Religious Studies, Law, Psychology, Management School, Sociology, English Institute for Cultural Research, Linguistics, History, Theatre Studies, Educational Research. Some of these are hybrids themselves.

It is, of course, pure science that is missing. It is true that Gender and Technology does feature amongst the topics offered, but as we shall see this is presented and researched very much from the point of view of sociologists, rather than technologists. The absence of pure science in women's studies courses is commonplace in, what are becoming, established taught courses, particularly in the UK. However, in Germany, and in other countries, there are institutions that do address the problems of gender and science from a point of view that is more balanced between science and social science, for example, the Kompetenzzentrum Genderforschung in Informatik und Naturwissenschaften [GIN] at the University of Freiburg.

10.4 Disciplines and Skills: Opportunities and Problems

Traditionally universities have been organised along disciplinary lines. This long-standing structure and naming are a powerful legacy, even though what falls under these names is always changing rapidly. Students may well only study a subset of a discipline or specialty; practitioners, while they may say they are either trained in a particular discipline, say mathematics, or based in one, will undoubtedly specialise and also name themselves as experts in one or more specialties. The sense of belonging to a discipline can still be strong; it provides a base from which to branch out.

The prevalent notion of a discipline is one which prescribes boundaries and thereby defines an area of activity and subject matter. There is an assumption that within this area the same approach and modes of thinking will be successful. Thus a discipline enables practitioners to engage in disciplined thinking. So disciplines are enabling and productive. However, they are at the same time restrictive and confining. (Leitch 2000) Programmes such as women's studies highlight these tensions inherent in the notion of disciplinarity. On the one hand, a student needs training in a discipline (usually just one) on the other hand they must branch out into new academic disciplines and cross boundaries in order to get breadth of subject matter. In these programmes students have to learn something about methods in all sorts of disciplines and this leads to the creation of a cross-disciplinary knowledge base i.e. several different disciplinary skills in one person. This feature of interdisciplinarity should be viewed more as an opportunity than a problem.

However, there are potential problems in interdisciplinary learning. We must, of course, avoid producing 'Jacks of all trades and masters of none' or making the "naïve assumption that an interdisciplinary product will emerge spontaneously from mixing different disciplinarians in classrooms" (Klein 1996, p. 92). On the other hand, we cannot demand that faculty are polymathic and have a high level of skill in many disciplines.

This is not an easy balance to characterise, let alone maintain and get accepted by the academy.

10.5 Permeating Boundaries

As we have observed, interdisciplinary work is always at the boundaries. The emergence of interdisciplinarities from the permeation of disciplinary boundaries can occur for many reasons – for example, the realisation of a common understanding of natural phenomena provided by plate tectonics, or the development of new techniques following the discovery of the structure of DNA. It is worth, therefore, taking a closer look at the nature of these boundaries.

Some boundaries are more permeable than others. Within, say, the natural sciences the boundaries can be extremely porous. For plate tectonics the boundaries between at least four disciplines: geology, physics, chemistry and biology were all porous at the points on the boundary where they all wanted an explanation of movements in the earth's crust.

However, the so-called hard sciences physics, maths, chemistry and the hard pseudo-science of computing have almost impermeable boundaries; this is true with respect to the social sciences and most especially when a social scientist takes the initiative. Indeed they are virtually watertight at the boundaries between the natural sciences and gender and feminist studies.

However, feminist philosophers, such as Sandra Harding, try to make these boundaries more permeable. She talks mockingly of "Sacred Science" (Harding 1986). Science holds itself above and beyond other disciplines. A science like physics claims to exemplify an empirical method of investigation that will give a true explanation of any other form of social activity, but it will not subject itself to this method. In other words it is above its own law. Thus it does not allow attempts to explain scientific activity in the way that science itself recommends we explain all other social activity. But hypotheses about science's role in social affairs should be open to the same kind of investigation as physics itself uses.

> Yet these statements [hypotheses] appear blasphemous to the vast majority of both scientists and non-scientists – not bold hypotheses that should be scientifically investigated to determine whether or not they can be refuted but psychologically, morally, and politically threatening challenges to the Western faith in progress through increased empirical knowledge. (p. 38)

Harding continues

> Why is it taboo to suggest that natural science . . . is a social activity, a historically varying

set of social practices? that a *thoroughgoing* and *scientific* appreciation of science requires descriptions and explanations of the regularities and underlying causal tendencies of science's own social practices and beliefs? that scientists and science enthusiasts may have the least adequate understanding of the real causes and meanings of their own activities? To what other 'community of natives' would we give the final word about the causes, consequences, and social meanings of their own beliefs and institutions? (p. 39)

However, in reality making the boundaries permeable in this way is not that easy. In a footnote Harding reports an observation by Pauline Bart "that in speculating about the comparative resistances that different disciplinary fields offer to feminist insights, we should not underestimate the comparative levels of personal and political threat to the leaders of these fields – primarily men . . ." For example, in my own discipline of computer science, if I suggest that the theory of computer science might be socially constructed, I am invariably met with what my colleagues think is the unanswerable retort: 'But it's not computing!'. Harding then continues "This line of reasoning would support my argument that feminist critiques of the natural sciences meet even greater hostility than critiques in other areas, scientific rationality is directly implicated in the maintenance of masculinity in our kind of culture." (pp. 33–4) This suggests that it is the introduction of gender as well as the introduction of social science into the discussion that provokes the defensive closing of boundaries.[23]

These quotations from Harding go some way to explaining the impermeability of the boundaries between social sciences and the 'hard' sciences. Forces external to these sciences certainly have little effect. Moreover, there are plenty of internal boundary patrols hampering feminists already in the sciences trying to get to grips with these basic issues through interdisciplinary activity.

However, there is some 'pushing' on the interdisciplinary

boundaries between social sciences and some of these hard sciences in gender analyses of the way scientific and technological artefacts are used. I will give some examples.

We rate physics very highly, placing it above all other sciences, because of the intellectual content of theories like Einstein's theory of relativity. This makes physics the paradigm science and therefore the prime target for feminists including the theory on which its prestige rests. So some feminists mistakenly believe that they have to show that Einstein's theory is gender-biased – a difficult thing to demonstrate. Yet, of course, it is not difficult to show that physics as a social activity is shot through with gender bias. So we do not need to show that Einstein's theory is gender biased in order to know that the ratio of women to men in physics departments is very low. (Harding 1986)

In the life sciences it should be recognised that there is permeability, for example, resulting in the realisation of the relative importance of women's interests in sex related health issues (reproduction, menstruation etc.) and sex differences in the manifestation of heart disease. The quantifiable branches of psychology are another exception to this idea that the boundaries between social sciences and sciences (in this case statistics) are always watertight.

All this is more applicable to the basic elements of these sciences (e.g. physical theories, mathematical theorems, programming languages) than to the way in which they are used. It cannot be argued that the development of any of these basic elements is self-determining; they are all a product of social forces. For example, complexity theory was developed for computing, and computers are a product of war.

Now I shall give two examples from the boundary between computing and gender. The first is from Ruth Woodfield's book *Women, Work and Computing* (Woodfield 2000), in which she describes her research in a UK software organisation into the working lives of the men and women who worked in their Research and Development department during a period in the 1990s. The company tried to introduce a policy that valued so-called feminine virtues of good social skills with high quality technical (or 'male') skills. For various reasons this policy was not a great success and women finished up where they always had been.

The second example of gender and computing is Esther Ruiz Ben's study of the development of expertise and professionalisation in the software industry and its interaction with gender (Ruiz Ben 2002).

In both these examples it is clear that, in spite of improvements in numbers and policy changes in favour of women, their subordinate position is in fact, through complex processes, being reinforced.

For Sharon Traweek (Traweek 1988) in her anthropological study of high-energy physicists, the marginalisation of women and supremacy of men is a recurring theme. These studies are certainly taken seriously by members of the disciplines and specialties from which the authors come; however, I am not aware of much interest of the relevant literature on the part of computer scientists.

Participatory Design and Computer Supported Cooperative Work are both instances of now well-established specialties for which a starting point was the interaction between human users and various types of technology. All these, both the studies and the specialties, are examples of interdisciplinary activity.

10.6 Interdisciplinary 'Objects'

Working at the boundaries requires a focus or thematic area that can be referred to as 'an object'. The very notion of new 'objects' arising at the points of contact brings to mind some aspects of Foucault's notions of discourse. The word 'object' can easily get overloaded, so for the moment I shall use it in the way Foucault does, as in an 'object of discourse'. He uses it in the context of the appearance of 'madness' in the nineteenth century at the time of the birth of psychiatry. He describes rules of discursive formation that include rules for the construction of objects of discourse like madness. Such objects of discourse do not have an isolated existence. ". . . mental illness was constituted by all that was said in all the statements that named it, divided it up, described it, explained it, traced its developments, . . ., judged it." (Foucault 2002, p. 35). The intersection of the planes of the judiciary, medicine and the police creates a space in which mental illness came to be defined, or in which homicide came to be defined, say. It is therefore the relationship between these planes (at a point in time) in which mental illness is defined. In a similar way we could say that the interpretation or concept of 'plate tectonics' arose as an object of discourse at the intersection of the planes of geophysics, geology, geobiology and geochemistry.

In some cases new 'objects of study' arise around something identifiable that may already be signified by a name; an example would be the structure of DNA on which both biologists and physicists could focus, thus giving rise to molecular biology. At this point we need to recognise that we are using the term 'object' as in 'object of study' in a more traditional way than Foucault does. We are using it to refer to objects whose existence is understood by all the interacting planes of discipline. In some sense we can view molecular biology as a discourse that has been formed by the contributions, utterances, publications and so on of a range of physicists, chemists and biologists since the 1920s. (Keller 1993)

How can this interdisciplinary work with objects at the boundaries be done? The participating disciplines may well recognise that an object of study exists, but start by viewing it in different ways. Let us try to outline some steps using the example of a mathematical theorem. Can this be viewed both by a mathematician and, say, a historian each in their own way but simultaneously absorbing and somehow representing the view of the other? The story of Fermat's Last Theorem which was finally resolved in 1994 is described in a book of that name by Simon Singh (Singh 1998). It presents the history of this problem, the attempts to solve it and the hugely complex matter of its final resolution. Students of mathematics are rarely required to study such background information to a theorem in order to make science plausible. But they should have this together with a comprehensible version of the proof. If we are to create a credible science and not leave mathematics at "the far end of the continuum of value-laden inquiry traditions" (Harding 1986, p. 47) this kind of pluralism has to be established as scientific activity. [24]

The argument that such presentations of scientific work are merely 'populist' seldom comes with much justification or any further discussion about how such derogatory labels are justified.

I'm not suggesting that accounts of this type provide the solution to this problem of expanding the meaning of science, but they give rise to new ideas and discussion. Foucault's objects of discourse are defined within the context of what discourse is. "Discourse is not about objects: rather, discourse constitutes them." (Sheridan 1980, p. 98). So if we use 'discourse' in this Foucauldian sense, Fermat's Last Theorem is not an object of discourse, it is merely an object of study. We do not know, yet, what the object of discourse is in this case. It might be the emergence of 'something' new: a new interdisciplinary concept, or perhaps even a new discipline.

Additionally, there are other steps in interdisciplinary work, that are worth mentioning. The *use* of a common tool can also be classified as a *boundary activity*. Techniques, tools and methods can be shared across interdisciplinary boundaries and, possibly, adapted in the process. Susan Leigh Star and James R. Griesemer, in their analysis of the creation of Berkeley's Museum of Vertebrate Zoology, also talk of *boundary objects*. "These are objects which are plastic enough to adapt to local needs and the constraints of the several parties employing them, yet robust enough to maintain a common identity across sites" (Star & Griesemer 2016, p. 393). There were professionals (biologists and administrators) and amateurs (trappers, farmers and collectors) all participating in collecting specimens of flora and fauna to record for posterity what existed in California in the early 20th century. They shared a common goal: "preserve California's nature", although they may have had different motives for achieving this. The museum, a repository for their collections, was one boundary object. Another object that emerged in this exercise was "Standardized forms. . . devised as methods of common communication across dispersed work groups" or agreed tools; a form they had to complete that standardised the way in which information was collected.

Naming is another crucial boundary activity. I use the word 'naming' to refer to both the signified and the signifier. If interdisciplinary boundaries are impermeable, this can arise in part from unintentional or intentional misunderstandings about names, about what is signified (be it a concept, an object (in any sense of that word) or an activity) and the way it is being described. If the discipline on one side of the boundary, say physics, mathematics or computing, is resistant to the interdisciplinary activities of the discipline on the other side, then there may well be overuse of unexplained technical or scientific jargon.

10.7 Fragment the Disciplines?

Somehow these boundaries have to become more permeable. The boundary patrols exert a definite resistance to change – a resistance that has in turn to be resisted. Presumably this can be achieved in the Foucauldian tradition of small local struggles or capillary resistance and the creation of as many interdisciplinary points of contact as possible.

If the control that disciplines currently exert on us is to be weakened, we must aim for increasing the fragmentation of disciplines. This could be aided by withdrawing from the constraining effect of seeing ourselves as mono-disciplinarians. Multi-disciplinarity for all should be encouraged so that our allegiances are always fundamentally divided.

Vincent Leitch (Leitch 2000) concludes his paper, entitled Postmodern Interdisciplinarity in a way I would be rash to try and improve on

While I believe that North American college and university professors are disciplinary subjects, that our universities are disciplinary institutions serving disciplinary societies, and that interdisciplinary enterprises tend to buttress the disciplines, I also know that innumerable local subversions, creative misuses, and antidisciplinary moves continuously loosen the rigidities and holds of the modern disciplinary system. And too, interdisciplinary projects – whether inside, between, or among disciplines – frequently increase permeabilities and deterritorialize fixed cognitive maps.

EPILOGUE

The role and effect of social media has not been addressed in this collection. These are now in 2020 hugely influential; the effects they are having and will have on women inside and outside the world of computing are beginning to emerge. (See for a start this Wikipedia entry on gender differences in social network use.[25]) When I started compiling this book I was reviewing what had arisen during my working life, it was not possible at that time to speculate about how this massive development would affect women and men – indeed it is extremely difficult even now.

Mores (rules as to what is acceptable or unacceptable) depend on local social customs and traditions; these are also influenced by legislation, political and religious rules, universal human rights and international agreements. The new media are instrumental in the changes that are occurring to these mores - standards and protocols are constantly evolving and boundaries between existing cultures are shifting. New developments in communication and so on will encourage cultures to have new identities – national identity, gender identity and racial identity could well become beliefs of the past. We have yet to see how all this will develop. It could become an object of discourse where planes of interest intersect (see Section 10.6) and even become a new discipline in itself.

It is evident that, so far, the major digital platforms who facilitate these changes, have not been really interested in equality or preventing abuse and suffering – as opposed to acting proactively – they react to damaging events as they occur. They have not endeavoured to prevent or to stop trolling, on-line harassment in the form of on-line sexism, racism and so on. Controls on those who host these platforms are still in a state of flux as the debate on freedom of expression rages in the wider world. The platform holders are only now being asked, and possibly forced, to take notice of detrimental effects. This question about what manner of controls there should be applied to the users of these platforms as well as the owners and developers remains to be determined.

The things that they are always quite good at selling are the benefits! And indeed, there are huge benefits to be had in so many ways; to mention just two: speed of communicating with friends and extending networks and, in short, learning so much. But we should be wary that there could be lurking behind these seemingly golden benefits opportunities for misuse.

The OECD has recently produced a timely and comprehensive report (OECD 2019) entitled *The Role of Education and Skills in Bridging the Digital Gender Divide*. It reports on factors which inhibit the progress of women with particular emphasis on and reports from APEC countries. This means that data is presented not just from the usual western sources but from more countries where women have extra disadvantages from lack of access to digital technology and in which societies are often unaware of restraints on women's requirements. The range of influential factors covered in this report (including of course the cyber bullying mentioned above, family influences, demand for domestic work and so on – in fact it's difficult to see what's missing) is extremely impressive.

It is to be hoped that readers will reflect on the multiplicity of ways in which those matters included in the preceding chapters as well as the OECD report are likely to have on future developments. Hopefully readers will recall how the ground was in so many ways well prepared for much of what we are experiencing now and particularly in respect of 'Gender Gaps'. There is no one organisation to which we can apportion blame. This happened because of the rapid development of technology within a misogynistic and sexist environment.

We must be more aware of the new foundations now being created and do the best we can to watch carefully new developments and ponder the effects they are having on us personally and accommodate all those with whom we come into contact. We must, whenever necessary, speak out and ensure that we are heard.

REFERENCES

50th Anniversary Celebrations. (1997). Retrieved 2020-02-04, from http://curation.cs.manchester.ac.uk/computer50/

Ada Lovelace Online (2020). Retrieved 2020-08-19, from https://findingada.com/events/ada-lovelace-day-live/

Ada Lovelace Festival (2020). Retrieved 2020-02-04, from http://wiwo.konferenz.de/ada/en/

Anon. (1834). On the Connexion of the Physical Sciences. by Mrs Somerville. *The Quarterly Review, L1,* 54–68. Retrieved 2020-02-04, from https://babel.hathitrust.org/cgi/pt?id=mdp.39015074711394;view=1up;seq=60

Association for Women in Mathematics (2020). Retrieved 2020-07-23 from https://awm-math.org/awards/kovalevsky-lectures/

Audain, C. (1998). *Florence Nightingale.* Retrieved 2018-06-05, from http://www.agnesscott.edu/lriddle/women/nitegale.htm

Bacon, F. (1858). *The Works of Francis Bacon* Vol. IV. (J. Spedding, R. Ellis, & D. Heath, Eds.).London: Longmans and Co. Retrieved from http://archive.org/details/worksfrancisbac00heatgoog

BCS – The Chartered Institute for IT. (2018). Retrieved 2018-06-02, from https://www.bcs.org/

Beard, M. (2017). *Women & Power: A Manifesto.* London: Profile Books : London Review of Books.

Bennett, M. (2017, August 24). *GCSE results highlight growing gender gap in technology subjects.* Retrieved 2018-05-24, from https://

government.diginomica.com/2017/08/24/gcse-results-highligh
t-growing-gender-gap-technology-subjects/

Bizzabo. (2020) *Women In Tech Conferences: Empowering Events.*
Retrieved 2020-02-18, from https://blog.bizzabo.com/women-in-
technology-conferences

Bjorkman, C., Chrisoff, I., Palm, F., & Vallin, A. (1997). Exploring the
Pipeline: Towards an Understanding of the Male Dominated
Computing Culture and its Influence on Women. In R. Lander & A.
Adam (Eds.), *Women in Computing* (pp. 50–59). Exeter: Intellect Ltd.

Boole, G. (1854). *An Investigation of the Laws of Thought: On which are
Founded the Mathematical Theories of Logic and Probabilities.* London:
Walton and Maberly. (Google-Books-ID: DqwAAAAAcAAJ)

Booth, R., & Hern, A. (2017, August). Google employee fired over diversity
row considers legal action. *The Guardian.* Retrieved 2020-02-04,
from http://www.theguardian.com/technology/2017/aug/08/
google-employee-fired-diversity-row-considers-legal-action-j
ames-damore

Boyle, R. (1664). *Experiments and Considerations Touching Colours* (Kindle
ed.). Amazon.

Bratky, S. L. (1988). Foucault, Femininity and the Modernization of
Patriarchal Power. In I. Diamond & L. Quinby (Eds.), *Feminism
& Foucault: Reflections on Resistance* (pp. 61–86). Northeastern
University Press. (Google-Books-ID: imcHngEACAAJ)

Brockes, E. (2017, November). Weinstein has done what Trump couldn't:
unite feminists Emma Brockes. *The Guardian* .Guardian, The Retrieved
2020-02-04, from http://www.theguardian.com/commentisfree/2017/
nov/16/ weinstein-trump-feminists-sexual-harassment

Bromley, A. G. (1990, December). Difference and Analytical Engines.
In W. Asprey (Ed.), *Computing Before Computers* (pp. 59–98). www.
uipress.uiowa.edu: Iowa State University Press.

Brooks, F. P. (1996, March). The computer scientist as toolsmith II.
Communications of the ACM, 39(3), 61–68. Retrieved 2018-05-30,

from http://portal.acm.org/citation.cfm?doid=227234.227243 doi: 10.1145/227234.227243

Camp, T. (1997, October). The Incredible Shrinking Pipeline. *Communications of the ACM, 40*(10), 103–110. Retrieved 2018-05-30, from http://portal.acm.org/citation.cfm?doid=262793.262813 doi: 10.1145/262793.262813

CAS (2018). *Computing At School.* Retrieved 2018-06-03, from https://www.computingatschool.org.uk/about

Chalmers, A. F. (1999). *What is this Thing Called Science?* (3rd ed.). Maidenhead, UK: Open University Press.

Chang, E. (2018). *Brotopia: Breaking Up the Boys' Club of Silicon Valley.* New York, New York: Portfolio Penguin.

Clark, K. (1992, January). The Linguistics of Blame: Representation of Women in the *Sun* Reporting of Crimes of Sexual Violence. In M. J. Toolan (Ed.), *Language, Text and Context: Essays in Stylistics* (pp. 94–122). Routledge. (Google-Books-ID: N94OAAAAQAAJ)

Cockburn, C. (1983). *Brothers: Male Dominance and Technological Change.* University of Michigan: Pluto Press.

Cockburn, C. (1988). *Machinery of Dominance: Women, Men and Technical Know-how.* London : Dover, N.H: Northeastern University Press.

Cohn, C. (1996). Nuclear Language and How We Learned to Pat the Bomb. In E. F. Keller & H. E. Longino (Eds.), *Feminism and Science.* Oxford University Press, USA.

Council of Economic Advisers. (2000, May 11). *Opportunities and Gender Pay Equity in New Economic Occupations.* Retrieved 2018-06-06, from https://clintonwhitehouse4.archives.gov/media/pdf/payequitypaperfinal.pdf

Coy, W. (1997). Defining discipline. In C. Freksa, M. Jantzen, & R. Valk (Eds.), *Foundations of Computer Science: Potential — Theory — Cognition* (pp. 21–35). Berlin, Heidelberg: Springer Berlin Heidelberg.

Retrieved 2018-10-14, from https://doi.org/10.1007/BFb0052074 doi: 10.1007/BFb0052074

Damore, J. (2017, July). *Google's Ideological Echo Chamber.* Retrieved 2018-06-18, from https://www.documentcloud.org/documents/3914586-Googles-Ideological-Echo-Chamber.html

de Beauvoir, S. (1988). *The Second Sex* (H. M. Parshley, Ed.). London: Pan Books Ltd.

Denning, P. J., Comer, D. E., Gries, D., Mulder, M. C., Tucker, A., Turner, A. J., & Young, P. R. (1988). Report of the ACM Task Force on The Core of Computer Science. *Communications of the ACM.*

Denning, P. J., Comer, D. E., Gries, D., Mulder, M. C., Tucker, A., Turner, A. J., & Young, P. R. (1989, January). Computing as a discipline. *Communications of the ACM, 32*(1), 9–23. Retrieved 2018-05-29, from http://portal.acm.org/citation.cfm?doid=63238.63239 doi: 10.1145/63238.63239

Devlin, H. (2017, August 20). Two-year-olds should learn to code, says computing pioneer. *The Guardian.* Retrieved 2018-05-24, from http://www.theguardian.com/technology/2017/aug/20/two-year-olds-should-learn-to-code-says-computing-pioneer

Diamond, I., & Quinby, L. (1988). *Feminism & Foucault: Reflections on Resistance.* Boston: Northeastern University Press. (Google-Books-ID: tqdkAAAAIAAJ)

Dijkstra, E. W. (1989, December). On the cruelty of really teaching computing science. *Communications of the ACM, 32*(12), 1397–1414. Retrieved 2018-05-29, from http://portal.acm.org/citation.cfm?doid=76380.76381 (Within A Debate on Teaching Computer Science, Denning et al) doi: 10.1145/76380.76381

Dorothy Vaughan. (2018, October). Retrieved 2018-10-20, from https://en.wikipedia.org/wiki/Dorothy Vaughan (Page Version ID: 863697906)

Easlea, B. (1980). *Witch Hunting, Magic and the New Philosophy: An Introduction to Debates of the Scientific Revolution 1450–1750.* Boston: Harvester Press.

Easlea, B. (1987). *Fathering the Unthinkable: Masculinity, Scientists and the Nuclear Arms Race.* Pluto Press.

Elephant in the Valley. (2017). Retrieved 2018-06-18, from https://www. elephantinthevalley.com/

engineer | Shorter Oxford English Dictionary. (1979). Oxford: Clarendon Press.

engineering | Merriam-Webster Dictionary. (2018). Retrieved 2018-05-30, from. https://www.merriam-webster.com/dictionary/engineering

ENIAC Programmers Project - Documentary Team. (2010). Retrieved 2018-06-18, from http://eniacprogrammers.org/documentary-info/ documentary-info/

EOC. (2001). *Facts about Women & Men in Great Britain 2001.* Retrieved 2018-06-22, from https://drive.google.com/drive/ folders/1WlO9RkewUuNScPFzqiO-ouEzgVDfzQUl

EOC. (2002). *Facts about Women & Men in Great Britain 2002.* Retrieved 2018-06-22, from https://drive.google.com/drive/ folders/1WlO9RkewUuNScPFzqiO-ouEzgVDfzQUl

–ette Oxford Dictionary Definition. (2014). Retrieved 2018-10-11, from https://en.oxforddictionaries.com/definition/us/–ette

Etzkowitz, H., Kemelgor, C., Neuschatz, M., Uzzi, B., & Alonzo, J. (1994, October). The paradox of critical mass for women in science. *Science, 266*(5182), 51–54. Retrieved 2018-06-07, from http://science. sciencemag.org/content/266/5182/51 doi: 10.1126/science.7939644

European Institute for Gender Equality. (2017). *Gender Equality Index 2017.* Retrieved 2018-05-24, from https://eige.europa.eu/ publications/gender-equality-index-2017-measuring-gender-equ ality-european-union-2005-2015-report

European Institute for Gender Equality. (2019). *Gender Equality Index 2019.* Retrieved 2020-05-17, from https://eige.europa.eu/publications/ gender-equality-index-2019-work-life-balance

Fairclough, N., & Wodak, R. (1997, March). Critical Discourse Analysis. In T. A. van Dijk (Ed.), *Discourse as Social Interaction: Discourse as Social Interactions v. 2* (1st ed., pp. 258–284). London: Sage Publications Ltd.

Fausto-Sterling, A. (2000). *Sexing the Body: Gender Politics and the Construction of Sexuality.* New York: Basic Books. (Google-Books-ID: c3lhYfZzIXkC)

Florman, S. C. (1996). *The Existential Pleasures of Engineering.* (2nd edition) New York: St. Martin's Press.

Foreman, D., Grundy, F., & Lees, S. (1997, June). Sex, Age and the Desirability of Computers. In A. F. Grundy, D. Köhler, U. Petersen, & V. Oechtering (Eds.), *Women, Work and Computerization: Spinning a Web from Past to Future* (pp.99–110). Springer.

Foucault, M. (1977). *Discipline and Punish: The Birth of the Prison.* London: Penguin Books. (Google-Books-ID: 0NT7ngEACAAJ)

Foucault, M. (1978). *I, Pierre Rivière, Having Slaughtered my Mother, my Sister, And my Brother.: A Case of Parricide in the Nineteenth Century.* Peregrine Books. Retrieved 2020-02-04, from https://www. amazon.co.uk/Pierre-Rivi\unhbox\ voidb@x\bgroup\let\unhbox\ voidb@x\setbox\@tempboxa\hbox{e\ global\mathchardef\accent@ spacefactor\spacefactor}\ accent18e\egroup\spacefactor\accent@ spacefactorre-Having-Slaughtered-Brother/dp/0140551255/ref=sr 1 cc 2?s=aps&ie=UTF8&qid=1528367265&sr=1–2–catcorr

Foucault, M. (1998). *The History of Sexuality: The Will to Knowledge Volume 1.* London: Penguin Books Ltd.

Foucault, M. (2002). *Archaeology of Knowledge.* London: Routledge Classics. (Google-Books-ID: kyKuUTYEn5sC)

Foucault, M., & Kritzman, L. D. (1988). *Politics, philosophy, culture: interviews and other writings, 1977–1984.* London : New York: Routledge. (Google-Books-ID: editions:iCLirnR9–QMC)

Freiberger, P. A., & Swaine, M. R. (2008, October). *ENIAC computer.* Retrieved 2018-06-18, from https://www.britannica.com/ technology/ENIAC

Fry, H. (2015). *Calculating Ada: The Countess of Computing.* Retrieved 2018-06-15, from https://www.bbc.co.uk/programmes/p030s5bx

GABe, F. (1983, February). The GABe Self-Cleaning House. In *The Technological Woman: Interfacing with Tomorrow* (pp. 75–82). Praeger Publishers Inc.

Gewirtz, M. L., & Lindsey, A. (2015). *Women in the New Economy: Insights & Realities.* Retrieved 2020-02-04, from https://www.slideshare.net/MindyLGewirtzPhD/ women-in-the-new-economy-insights-realities

Gibbons, M. (1994). *The New Production of Knowledge: The Dynamics of Science and Research in Contemporary Societies.* London : Thousand Oaks: New Delhi: SAGE

Gender differences on social media. (2020) Gender differences in social network service use. Retrieved 2020-02-22 from https://en.wikipedia.org/wiki/Gender_differences_in_social_network_service_use Wikipedia.

Gibbs, W. W. (1994, September). Software's Chronic Crisis. *Scientific American, 271*(3), 86–95. Retrieved 2020-02-04, from http://www.nature.com/doifinder/ 10.1038/scientificamerican0994-86 doi: 10.1038/scientificamerican0994–86

Gilligan, C. (1993). *In a Different Voice: Psychological Theory and Women's Development.* Cambridge, Massachusetts : London, England: Harvard University Press.

Glanvill, J. (1661). *The Vanity of Dogmatizing.* Retrieved 2020-02-04, from https://www.exclassics.com/glanvil/glanvil.pdf

Glover J. (2000). *Women and Scientific Employment.* Basingstoke, England and London: Macmillan Press Ltd. (Google-Books-ID: X6iHDAAAQBAJ)

Goldberger, N. R. (1998, April). Looking backward, looking forward. In N. R. Goldberger, J. M. Tarule, B. M. Clinchy, & M. F. Belenky (Eds.), *Knowledge, Difference, And Power: Essays Inspired By Women's Ways Of Knowing* (pp. 1–18). New York: Basic Books.

Gov.UK DfE. (2012, July). *'Harmful' ICT curriculum set to be dropped to make way for rigorous computer science.* Retrieved 2018-05-24, from https://www.gov.uk/ government/news/harmful-ict-curriculum-set-to-be-dropped-to-make-way-for-rigorous–computer-science

Gov.UK DfE. (2014). *GCSE AS and A level subject content for Computer Science.* Retrieved 2018-05-24, from https://assets.publishing. service.gov.uk/ government/uploads/system/uploads/attachment data/file/ 302105/A level computer science subject content.pdf

Gov.UK DfE. (2015, January). *Computer Science GCSE subject content.* Retrieved 2018-05-24, from https://www.gov.uk/government/ uploads/system/ uploads/attachment data/file/397550/GCSE subject content for computer science.pdf

Green, E., Hebron, S., & Woodward, D. (1990). *Women's Leisure, What Leisure?: A Feminist Analysis* (1990 ed.). Basingstoke, Hampshire: Palgrave Macmillan.

Grundy, F. (1996). *Women and Computers.* Exeter: Intellect Books.

Guardian. (2020). *Thousands of university workers strike across UK.* Retrieved 2020-02-21, from https://www.theguardian.com/education/2020/ feb/20/thousands-of-university-workers-strike-across-uk

Gupta, P. (2001, July). Growth scenario of IT industries in India. *Communications of the ACM, 44*(7), 40–41. Retrieved 2018-06-07, from http://portal.acm.org/citation.cfm?doid=379300.379308 doi: 10.1145/379300.379308

Hacker, S. (1989). *Pleasure, Power, and Technology: Some Tales of Gender, Engineering, and the Cooperative Workplace.* London: Unwin Hyman.

Hacker, S. (1990). 'Doing it the Hard Way': Investigations of Gender and Technology. In (chap. 1). London: Unwin Hyman. (Google-Books-ID: GyHtAAAAMAAJ)

Haigh, T. (2017). *CHM Live Working on ENIAC: Rethinking Innovation Myths with Author Thomas Haigh Computer History Museum.* Retrieved 2018-06-17, from http://www.computerhistory.org/ events/video/220/

Haigh, T., Priestley, M., & Rope, C. (2018). *ENIAC in Action (History of Computing): Making and Remaking the Modern Computer* (Reprint edition ed.). Cambridge, Mass : London: MIT Press.

Haraway, D. J. (1985). A Manifesto for Cyborgs: Science, Technology, and Socialist Feminism in the 1980s. *Socialist Review, 80*, 65–108.

Harding, S. G. (1986). *The Science Question in Feminism*. Ithaca: London: Cornell University Press. (Google-Books-ID: 27TrCuk4LRgC)

Hartmanis, J. (1995, March). On Computational Complexity and the Nature of Computer Science. *ACM Comput. Surv., 27*(1), 7–16. Retrieved 2020-02-04, from http://doi.acm.org/10.1145/214037.214040 doi: 10.1145/214037.214040

Hello World. (2018). Retrieved 2018-05-24, from https://helloworld.raspberrypi.org

Henrion, C. (1997). *Women in Mathematics: The Addition of Difference*. Bloomington : Indianapolis: Indiana University Press. (Google-Books-ID: uQsxhvZr12QC)

Henwood, F. (1996, June). WISE Choices? Understanding Occupational Decision-making in a Climate of Equal Opportunities for Women in Science and Technology. *Gender and Education, 8*(2), 199–214. Retrieved 2020-02-04, from https://doi.org/10.1080/09540259650038860 doi: 10.1080/09540259650038860

HESA. (2001). *Higher Education Student Statistics: UK, 2000/01 – Resources*. Retrieved 2020-06-04, from https://www.hesa.ac.uk/data-and-analysis/publications/resources-2000-01 Table 18a Full Time Academic Staff by Cost Centre and Gender

HESA. (2018a). *Higher Education Student Statistics: UK, 2016/17 – Qualifications achieved*. Retrieved 2018-05-24, from https://www.hesa.ac.uk/news/11-01-2018/sfr247-higher-education-student–statistics/qualifications

HESA. (2018b). *Higher Education Student Statistics: UK, 2016/17 – Subjects studied*. Retrieved 2018-05-24, from https://www.hesa.ac.uk/

news/11-01-2018/ sfr247-higher-education-student-statistics/ subjects

Hodges, A. (1992). *Alan Turing: The Enigma of Intelligence*. London: Vintage.

Information Age. (2016, August 26). Number of girls taking GCSE computing doubles. *Information Age*. Retrieved 2020-02-04, from http://www.information-age.com/number-girls-taking-gcse-computing-doubles–123461936/

JCQ. (2018). *Examination Results – 2015 - 2016*. Retrieved 2018-05-24, from https://www.jcq.org.uk/examination-results/

Jones, K. B. (1988). On Authority: Or, Why Women are not Entitled to Speak. In I. Diamond & L. Quinby (Eds.), *Feminism & Foucault: Reflections on Resistance* (pp. 119–134). Northeastern University Press. (Google-Books-ID: imcHngEACAAJ)

Katherine Johnson. (2020, June). Retrieved 2020-06-14, from https://en.wikipedia.org/wiki/Katherine_Johnson (Page Version ID: 864710922)

Keller, E. F. (1993). Fractured Images of Science, Language and Power: A Postmodern Optic or Just Bad Eyesight? In E. Messer-Davidow, D. R. Shumway, & D. Sylvan (Eds.), *Knowledges: Historical and Critical Studies in Disciplinarity* (pp. 54–69). University of Virginia Press. (Google-Books-ID: 0gCGl3aK2OIC)

Keller, E. F. (1995). *Reflections on Gender and Science: Tenth Anniversary Paperback Edition* (Anniversary edition ed.). New Haven : London: Yale University Press.

Kidder, T. (2011). *The Soul of a New Machine*. Hachette UK. (Google-Books-ID: oRg3AQAAQBAJ)

Klein, J. T. (1996). *Crossing Boundaries: Knowledge, Disciplinarities, and Interdisciplinarities*. Charlottesville : London: University of Virginia Press. (Google-Books-ID: bNJvYf3ROPAC)

Koblitz, A. H. (1983). *A Convergence of Lives: Sofia Kovalevskaia: Scientist, Writer, Revolutionary.* Basel : Boston: Birkhäuser. (Google-Books-ID: qHuWQQAACAAJ)

Lander, R., & Adam, A. (1997). *Women in Computing.* Intellect. (Google-Books-ID: EgFsQgAACAAJ)

Lee, D. (1992) *Competing Discourses: Perspective and Ideology in language.* Routledge.

Leitch, V. (2000). Postmodern interdisciplinarity. In *Profession 2000* (pp. 124–131). Modern Language Association of America.

Levy, S. (1984). *Hackers: Heroes of the Computer Revolution.* New York: Anchor Press/Doubleday.

Lloyd, G. (1984). *The Man of Reason: "Male" and "Female" in Western Philosophy.* Methuen.

Maibaum, T. S. E. (1997). What We Teach Software Engineers in the University: Do We Take Engineering Seriously? In *Proceedings of the 6th European SOFTWARE ENGINEERING Conference Held Jointly with the 5th ACM SIGSOFT International Symposium on Foundations of Software Engineering* (pp. 40–50). New York, NY, USA: Springer–Verlag New York, Inc.

Martin, B. (1988). Feminism, Criticism and Foucault. In I. Diamond & L. Quinby (Eds.), *Feminism & Foucault: Reflections on Resistance* (pp. 3–19). Northeastern University Press. (Google-Books-ID: imcHngEACAAJ)

Mary Jackson. (2018, October). Retrieved 20120-03-11, from https:// en.wikipedia.org/wiki/Mary_Jackson_(engineer) (Page Version ID: 864720645)

McHoul, A. W. (1997). *A Foucault Primer: Discourse, Power, and the Subject.* New York: New York University Press. (Google-Books-ID: fskaLgEACAAJ)

Merchant, C. (1990). The Death of Nature: Women, Ecology and the Scientific Revolution. HarperOne.

Mill, J. S. (1869). *The Subjection of Women*. London: Longmans, Green, Reader and Dyer. Retrieved 2017-11-04, from https://books.google.co.uk/books?id=XHwIAAAAQAAJ&printsec=frontcover&dq=the+subjection+women&hl=en&sa=X&ved=0ahUKEwj7r56vuqjZAhWBDsAKHeNtBFgQuwUILDAA#v=onepage&q&f= fals

Mill, J. S. (1970). The Subjection of Women. In A. S. Rossi (Ed.), *Essays on Sex Equality*. Chicago: University of Chicago Press.

Mill, J. S. (2009). *Autobiography of John Stuart Mill*. www.thefloatingpress.com: The Floating Press. (Google-Books-ID: 0qS6ND uct0C)

Möbius, P. J. (1907). *Über die Anlage zur Mathematik*. Leipzig: Johann Ambrosius Barth.

Neeley, K. A. (2001). *Mary Somerville: Science, Illumination, and the Female Mind*. Cambridge, England: Cambridge University Press.

Nicolson, P. (1996). *Gender, Power and Organisation*. London : New York: Routledge.

Oechtering, V., & Behnke, R. (1995, January). Situations and advancement measures in Germany. *Communications of the ACM*, *38*(1), 75–82. Retrieved 2018-07-29, from http://dl.acm.org/citation.cfm?doid=204865.204881 doi: 10.1145/204865.204881

OECD (2019). *The Role of Education and Skills in Bridging the Digital Gender Divide Evidence from APEC Economies*. Retrieved 2020-02-29, from http://www.oecd.org/going-digital/education-and-skills-in-bridging-the-digital-gender-divide-evidence-from-apec.pdf?utm_source=Adestra&utm_medium=email&utm_content=Download%20the%20report%20%28pdf%29&utm_campaign=OECD%20Science%2C%20Technology%20%26%20Innovation%20News%2002%2F2020&utm_term=demo

Parnas, D. L. (1997). Software Engineering (Extended): An Unconsummated Marriage. In *Proceedings of the 6th European SOFTWARE ENGINEERING Conference Held Jointly with the 5th ACM SIGSOFT International Symposium on Foundations of Software*

Engineering (pp. 1–3). New York, NY, USA: Springer–Verlag New York, Inc.

Patterson, E. C. (2012). *Mary Somerville and the Cultivation of Science, 1815–1840*. Springer Science & Business Media. (Google-Books-ID: yVtgBgAAQBAJ)

Peyton Jones, S. (2016, June 22). *Simon Peyton Jones – Computing at School – Part 1*. Retrieved 2018-05-24, from https://www.youtube.com/watch?v= RNKHN1zP24

Piper, L. (2017, 11). *Hidden secrets in new Scottish £10 banknote revealed*. Retrieved 2018-06-15, from https://stv.tv/news/features/1395439-hidden-secrets-in-new-scottish-10-banknote-revealed/

Poizat, B. (1987). *Groupes stables: une tentative de conciliation entre la géométrie algébrique et la logique mathématique*. Launay. (Google-Books-ID: JgjvAAAAMAAJ)

Rasmussen, B. (1997, June). Girls and computer science: "It's not me. I'm not interested in. . . ". In A. F. Grundy, D. Köhler, U. Petersen, & V. Oechtering (Eds.), *Women, Work and Computerization: Spinning a Web from Past to Future* (pp. 379–386). Springer.

Reddy, R. (1996, May). To dream the possible dream. *Communications of the ACM*, *39*(5), 105–112. Retrieved 2018-05-29, from http://portal.acm.org/citation.cfm?doid=229459.233436 doi: 10.1145/229459.233436

Ridley, L. (2015, January). *Bletchley Park: Meet 'Dilly's Girls', The WWII Women Codebreakers Who Cracked Enigma*. Retrieved 2018-06-17, from https://www.huffingtonpost.co.uk/2015/01/25/bletchley-park-enigma-female-codebreakers   n   6532856.html?guccounter=1

Riggins, S. H. (1997). *The Language and Politics of Exclusion: Others in Discourse*. Sage Publications. (Google-Books-ID: PVJiAAAAMAAJ)

Rogers, G. F. C. (1983). *The Nature of Engineering: A Philosophy of Technology*. London & Basingstoke: Macmillan Press. (Google-Books-ID: MUwhAQAAIAAJ)

Roper. (2001, June). *Women in Technology Leadership.* Retrieved 2019-02-03, from https://drive.google.com/drive/folders/1WlO 9RkewUuNScPFzqiO-ouEzgVDfzQUl

Rossi Becker, J. (1995, January). Women's Ways of Knowing in Mathematics. In P. Rogers & G. Kaiser (Eds.), *Equity in Mathematics Education: Influences of Feminism and Culture* (pp. 163–174). Falmer Press. (Google-Books-ID: editions:NARG7AkHOmYC)

Royal Society. (2012, January). *Shut down or restart? The way forward for computing in UK schools.* Retrieved 2018-05-24, from https://royalsociety.org/-/media/education/computing-in-schools/2012-01-12-computing-in-schools.pdf

Royal Society. (2017, November). *After the reboot: computing education in UK schools.* Retrieved 2018-05-24, from https://royalsociety.org/~/media/policy/projects/ computing-education/computing-education-report.pdf

Ruiz Ben, E. (2002). Qualifikation, erfahrung und geschlecht. *FiFFKo, 9,* 34–37.

Russell Group. (2013). *A Russell Group guide to making decisions about post–16 education.* Retrieved 2018-05-24, from https://issuu.com/russellgroup/docs/informedchoices-latest

Saujani, R. (2017). *Girls Who Code: Learn to Code and Change the World.* London: Virgin Books.

Saujani, R. (2018). *Girls Who Code.* Retrieved 2020-06-015, from https://girlswhocode.com/

Schiebinger, L. (1991). *The Mind Has No Sex?: Women in the Origins of Modern Science.* Cambridge Massachusetts: Harvard University Press. (Google-Books-ID:TqsVHasTHOYC)

Schiebinger, L. (1999). *Has Feminism Changed Science?* Cambridge Massachusetts: Harvard University Press.

Schinzel, B. (1997, June). Why has female participation in German informatics decreased? In A. F. Grundy, D. Köhler, U. Petersen, & V.

Oechtering (Eds.), *Women, Work and Computerization: Spinning a Web from Past to Future* (pp.365–378). Springer.

Schwartz Cowan, Ruth. (1983). *More Work for Mother: The Ironies of Household Technology from the Open Hearth to the Microwave*. New York: Basic Books.

Sheppard, A. (2013, October). *Meet the 'Refrigerator Ladies' Who Programmed the ENIAC*. Retrieved 2020-02-04, from http://mentalfloss.com/article/53160/ meet-refrigerator-ladies-who-programmed-eniac

Sheridan, A. (1980). *Michel Foucault: The Will to Truth*. London: Routledge. (Google-Books-ID: COrWAAAAMAAJ)

Shetterly, M. L. (2017). *Hidden Figures: The Untold Story of the African American Women Who Helped Win the Space Race*. William Collins.

Singh, S. (1998). *Fermat's Last Theorem: The Story of a Riddle that Confounded the World's Greatest Minds for 358 Years*. Fourth Estate.

Somerville, M. F. (2016). *Personal Recollections from Early Life to Old Age of Mary Somerville*. Library of Alexandria. (Google-Books-ID: wXxgDQAAQBAJ)

Star, S. L., & Griesemer, J. R. (2016, June). Institutional Ecology, 'Translations' and Boundary Objects: Amateurs and Professionals in Berkeley's Museum of Vertebrate Zoology, 1907–39. *Social Studies of Science*. Retrieved 2018-06-13, from http://journals.sagepub.com/doi/pdf/10.1177/ 030631289019003001 doi: 10.1177/030631289019003001

Stepulevage, L., & Plumeridge, S. (1998, September). Women Taking Positions Within Computer Science. *Gender and Education, 10*, 313–326. Retrieved 2018-06-01, from http://www.tandfonline.com/doi/abs/10.1080/09540259820925 doi: 10.1080/09540259820925

Thiel, P. (2009, April). *The Education of a Libertarian*. Retrieved 2018-06-18, from https://www.cato-unbound.org/2009/04/13/peter-thiel/education-libertarian

Timeline. (2017, May). *Women pioneered computer programming. Then men took their industry over.* Retrieved 2018-06-17, from https:// timeline.com/women-pioneered-computer-programming-then-men-took-their-industry-over-c2959b822523

Tonso, K. L. (1999). Engineering Gender-Gendering Engineering: A Cultural Model for Belonging. *Journal of Women and Minorities in Science and Engineering, 5*(4). Retrieved 2018-07-29, from http://www. dl.begellhouse.com/journals/ 00551c876cc2f027,0b16774275596e ac,0e4278055865732c.html doi:10.1615/JWomenMinorScienEng. v5.i4.60

Toole, B. A. (1998). *Ada: The Enchantress of Numbers: Prophet of the Computer Age, a Pathway to the 21st Century.* Strawberry Press. (Google-Books-ID: gnvZAAAAMAAJ)

Traweek, S. (1992). *Beamtimes and Lifetimes: The World of High Energy Physicists.* Harvard University Press.

Turing, A. M. (1950). I.—Computing Machinery and Intelligence. *Mind, LIX*(236), 433–460. Retrieved 2018-05-30, from https://academic. oup.com/mind/ article-lookup/doi/10.1093/mind/LIX.236.433 doi: 10.1093/mind/LIX.236.433

Turner, E. (1997, June). What is our Worth? In A. F. Grundy, D. Köhler, U. Petersen, &V. Oechtering (Eds.), *Women, Work and Computerization: Spinning a Web from Past to Future* (pp. 247–258). Springer.

Ullman, E. (1997). *Close to the Machine: Technophilia and its Discontents.* City Lights Books. (Google-Books-ID: D44fAQAAIAAJ)

Vaughan, T. (1919). *The Works of Thomas Vaughan* (A. E. Waite, Ed.). Retrieved from http://www.phoenixmasonry.org/Works-of-Thomas–Vaughan.pdf

Vehviläinen, M. (1997, June). Gender and Expertise in Retrospect: Pioneers of Computing in Finland. In A. F. Grundy, D. Köhler, U. Petersen, & V. Oechtering (Eds.), *Women, Work and Computerization: Spinning a Web from Past to Future.* (p. 235–248). Springer.

von Hellens, L., & Nielsen, S. (2001, July). Australian Women in ITo. *Communications of the ACM, 44*(7), 46–52. Retrieved 2018-06-06, from http://portal.acm.org/citation.cfm?doid=379300.379310 doi: 10.1145/379300.379310

Wajcman, J. (1991). *Feminism* Confronts *Technology* (Soft Cover; margin Notes edition ed.). University Park, Pa: Penn State Press.

Wegner, P. (1997, May). Why interaction is more powerful than algorithms. *Communications of the ACM, 40*(5), 80–91. Retrieved 2018-05-29, from http://portal.acm.org/citation.cfm?doid=253769.253801 doi: 10.1145/253769.253801

West, C., Lazar, M. M., & Kramarae, C. (1997, March). Gender in discourse. In T. A. van Dijk (Ed.), *Discourse as Social Interaction: Discourse as Social Interactions vol. 2* (1st ed., pp. 119–143). London: Sage Publications Ltd.

Whitby, B. (1996). *Reflections on Artificial Intelligence*. Exeter: Intellect.

White, M. (1998). *Isaac Newton: The Last Sorcerer*. Fourth Estate.

Whitehouse, C. (1997, February 14). Byte code with a Y chromosome. *The Times Higher Educational Supplement*.

Wodak, R. (1997). *Gender and Discourse*. SAGE. Retrieved 2018-07-29, from https://uk.sagepub.com/en-gb/eur/gender-and-discourse/book205373

Wolffensperger, J. (1993, January). 'Science Is Truly a Male World.' The Interconnectedness of Knowledge, Gender and Power within University Education. *Gender and Education, 5*(1), 37–54. Retrieved 2018-07-29, from https://doi.org/10.1080/0954025930050103 doi: 10.1080/0954025930050103

Women in Bletchley Park. (2018, September). Retrieved 2018-10-15, from https://en.wikipedia.org/w/index.php?title=Women_in_Bletchley_Park&oldid=858917370 (Page Version ID: 858917370)

Woodfield, R. (2000). *Women, Work and Computing*. Cambridge, UK; New York, NY, USA: Cambridge University Press.

Woolf, V. (1993). *A Room of One's Own/Three Guineas* (M. Bartlett, Ed.). London: Penguin Books.

Woolley, B. (1999). *The Bride of Science: Romance, Reason and Byron's Daughter*. Macmillan. (Google-Books-ID: editions:AHRXEuIGlHsC)

INDEX

ENDNOTES

1   I still recall during the period I was writing these papers hearing of remarks like "Can't we get Frances to stop writing these things?" being reported to me. And the editor of one prestigious US academic journal responded to the abstract for one of these papers saying that it was not suitable for his journal "nor any other computer journal". My then head of department offered to write to this editor on my behalf, but subsequently retracted his offer saying that he himself might want something published in the journal.

2   There is a reasonable objection to the use of the word 'coding' in connection with attracting the young to computing as expressed for example in the YouTube video (Peyton Jones 2016). There is a danger of hanging students on a 'hook of programming' that discourages creativity.

3   See for example Coderdojo (https://coderdojo.com/) 'The global network of free computer programming clubs for young people'. This is not for 2-year-olds but for children aged 7–17. Then there is Scratch (https://scratch.mit.edu/) which offers resource packs for games for use in primary computing education.

4   The YouTube videos introducing and explaining the commendable goals of CAS and the new curriculum while they frequently say 'every child' can perform certain activities but not one mention is made of the gender gap. (Peyton Jones 2016)

5   Data published in Women and Computers (Grundy 1996, Appendix A) shows something parallel but quite a bit better considering how long ago it was. For a cohort progressing from GCSE to taking A level 2 years later, in 1990 39.5% of the cohort sitting the GCSE exam were girls, then in 1992 only 17.3% of those who sat the A level were girls, of whom 15.8% passed.

6   In fact, prior to the 2014 curriculum change A-level computing was not accepted as a bona-fide A-level subject. This policy was reversed following a statement of policy change in 'Informed Choices' published by the Russell Group of Universities (Russell Group 2013)

7   This general index reflects an amalgam of trends in seven aspects of peoples' lives: power, time, money, knowledge, work health and violence.

8   Words such as these were in regular use in the 1980s and 90s amongst those running the computer systems and I have little doubt that, given their widespread use in that community, I probably used them myself from time to time.

9   Section 146(1)(b) of the Trade Union and Labour Relations (Consolidation) Act 1992

10 The RAE was replaced by the Research Excellence Framework (REF) in 2014.

11 Quality Assurance ratings for teaching were 'excellent', 'satisfactory', or 'unsatisfactory'. 'Excellent' was relatively rare. There is now a Quality Assurance Agency to check standards and quality.

12 In Britain, not only does the level of funding from central sources depend on the quality of research, it also depends on the *type* of subject taught. The more 'laboratory based' a subject is, the higher the level of funding for undergraduate teaching. Computer science has, for example, recently been upgraded from a 'half-lab' subject to a 'full-lab' subject thereby increasing its income for each undergraduate enrolled. So, there are strong financial incentives to calling the rooms where students work 'laboratories'.

13 This is to ignore the complication that, as I have argued in Chapter 3, computing is not a 'science' because it does not directly investigate objects in the real world.

14 The importance of this kind of consideration was underlined by John Stuart Mill in his essay, The Subjection of Women. "In all things of any difficulty and importance, those who can do them well are fewer than the need, even with the most unrestricted latitude of choice: and any limitation of the field of selection deprives society of some chances of being served by the competent, without ever saving it from the incompetent" (Mill 1970, p. 145)

15 Florence Nightingale (1820–1910). The two achievements for which she is best known are her pioneering of nursing and the reform of hospitals. What is less well known is how she developed and used statistical techniques to draw attention to the needless deaths caused by unsanitary conditions in the Crimean war. See for example (Audain 1998)

16 And at the time of this publication it's 40 years!

17 The introduction of word 'scientist' at this point seems to have occurred with more justification and meaningful discussion than occurred when the word 'science' was appended to computing 150 or so years later. Although expanding the meaning of a term is possibly easier so long as proponents are aware of the implications and the new contexts.

18 Russian women at this time were completely dependent on their father or husband and could not live apart from them without express permission. To circumvent this, women like Sofia, whose father would never have given permission for her to study abroad, would ask a man to marry them, then

would enter a 'fictitious marriage' so that they could travel abroad to study. Once abroad they could go their separate ways but did not always do so – Sofia did not but her marriage did not end happily.

19 These were two cipher systems used by the German military to transmit coded messages. Both were 'cracked' by code breakers at Bletchley Park greatly assisting the Allied war effort. Enigma was declassified in the 1970's and Lorenz was not declassified until 2002.

20 The bombe was an electro mechanical device used to decipher messages encrypted on the German Enigma machines. Alan Turing assisted in the design of this machine. Colossus refers to a set of computers that used thermionic valves or vacuum tubes, there were 10 in total by the end of the war. They were used to help decrypt the Lorenz code.

21 This reference includes a link to an on-line copy of the 1869 publication of this book which he completed in 1861 following the death of his wife Harriet Taylor Mill in 1858. Many other publications of this are available, for example, (Mill 1970). Scholars have argued about whether JS Mill or Harriet Taylor Mill wrote it, but it is generally thought he was the sole author, 'But all that is most striking and profound in what was written by me belongs to my wife.' (Mill 2009).

22 This has been going on for ever, see for example Angela Martin's cartoon included in my book (Grundy 1996, p. 76)

23 Recall the quotation from Sally Hacker in Chapter 4 that social scientists 'stand on their faces'.

24 Andrew Hodges' book on Alan Turing (Hodges 1992) provides a similar example.

25 https://en.wikipedia.org/wiki/Gender_differences_in_social_network_service_use